CW00494860

KEEP WALKING WITH GOD

Experiencing the realities of God amid challenging times

LOLA OSIKOYA

Copyright © Lola Osikoya, 2021

Without limiting the rights under copyright reserved above, no part of this publication may be reproduced stored in or introduced into retrieval system, or transmitted, in any form or by any means (electronic, mechanical, photocopying, recording, or otherwise), without the prior written permission of both the copyright owner and the publisher of this book.

The scanning, uploading, and distributing of this book via the Internert or via any other maens without permission of the publisher is illegal and punishable by law. Please purchase only authorized electronic editions and do not participate in or encourage electronic piracy of copyrightable material. Your support of the author's rights is appreciated immersely. Thanks and blessings!

ISBN: 9798759247104

Table of Contents

Except otherwise stated, all scriptures are taking from the King James Version of the Holy Bible.

Acknowledgements

I would love to acknowledge God Almighty who gave me the Holy Spirit and the wisdom to write this book. May Glory and Honor be to His name.

I would love to appreciate Pastor Daniel Ngerem, Minister Gilda Rochester, Funmi Omotayo, Prophet Eloi Aho, Minister Blandine Aho, Miss Tomi Omotayo, and my amazing children, Pastor Chinedu Igbokwe, Mrs. Shade Owoseje, Mr. Olujide Ogundeji, Miss Olamide Osikoya (MRS. Abidemi), Mrs. Bolanle Ogundeji, Mr. Ayodeji Osikoya, and to every leader, pastor, partner and member of the New Glory International Ministries. Your sacrifices in my life have been tremendous and you push me to become the best of myself. Each one of you have helped grow and exercise my potential. Thanks and you know I love you all!

Dedication

I dedicate this book to Stephen Howgego who has been on me each day to write a book. It is his nudges that made me exercise faith in this regard. He saw what I couldn't see. You are a leader and I appreciate the possibilities you saw in me. I encourage you to challenge more people to find their purpose and calling in this life. You are blessed!

I also want to dedicate this book to you my reader and to anyone overburden with the challenges of this life. It is my faith that in this

3

book you will find the faith to believe in God again in the midst of the challenges in and around you. Out of the challenges and hardness, you will discover purpose and God. And above all, I believe you will find your gift and use it to bless others in this world. God bless you as you spend time reading this book.

INTRODUCTION

L ife brings us diverse challenges each day. The problem is that when many people face this, they begin to lose faith and confidence in God. We are in a time where the world is going through crises and diverse challenges. There are economic, social, spiritual, financial, marriage, and even business crises all over the world now. In the midst of these crises, many people turn to lose their faith in God. Instead of believing, many focus on the challenges.

It is wrong to live life seeing the mountains and not the God of the mountains. It is wrong to live life focusing on what you are dealing with to a point that you are not seeing God and what He can do in your life. God's vision for the church—and even the world is to bring them to the place of absolute faith and trust in Him. You see, God never wants to find Himself in that position where He is going to combat for your faith. What He does to remedy the situation is that He puts you in circumstances that will wear off your human abilities and powers so that you can keep your faith in Him.

When we look at the life of Abraham, we can see a great insight into His life. He lived his life believing in God for a child. This didn't come early at all. As he lived, he had to learn to believe God in the midst of the hardness and challenges as well. This faith is what made him experience the realities of God. His faith in his walk with God invited the fullness of God to his realm.

Just imagine the kind of taunting and mockery he possibly was going through. He was dealing with this issue for not one year, but seventy-five years. But we can see that Abraham didn't allow his circumstances to shift him from the faith. He kept walking with God—*knowing that the One who promised was greater than His circumstances*. This made God allow the scriptures to carry the chronicles of his faith for our learning.

"Therefore [it is] of faith, that [it might be] by grace; to the end the promise might be sure to all the seed; not to that only which is of the law, but to that also which is of the faith of Abraham; who is the father of us all, (As it is written, I have made thee a father of many nations,) before him whom he believed, [even] God, who quickeneth the dead, and calleth those things which be not as though they were. Who against hope believed in hope, that he might become the father of many nations; according to that which was spoken, So shall thy seed be. And being not weak in faith, he considered not his own body now dead, when he was about an hundred years old, neither yet the deadness of Sara's womb: He staggered not at the promise of God through unbelief; but was strong in faith, giving glory to God; And being fully persuaded that, what he had promised, he was able also to perform. And therefore it was imputed to him for righteousness."—(Romans 4:16—22)

This text reveals and confirms the assertion I am making here. Looking at Abraham, he had every reason to be angry in life or even disappointed in life because everything was against him. Watching his wife each day weep and cry wanting a child was powerful enough to break him down. However, that didn't deter him out of faith. He rather was strong in the faith and believed God.

When the Lord began to deal with Abraham, the first thing God did was that He made him to shift his eyes from the circumstances so that Abraham could believe Him. The first thing God began to do was to begin to talk to Abraham as if it had happened already. This was the trigger for him—and he believed in God. The reward was that God credited to him as righteousness. Now we can agree with Paul where he said that righteousness comes through faith. Abraham became righteous by believing in God. We can as well become righteous by believing in God.

God began to call and point out the very things that He had intentions to do with Abraham as if it had happened. Romans 4:17 gives us that insight. God called the very things that are not as though they were. In other words, even though Abraham didn't have a child, God was seeing him as having a child. This was so real that it got Abraham to believe in God.

As God pointed him to the reality in the spirit, he also got the faith which made him see what God was showing him. This didn't just only bring him the reality of that realm, it made him become a disburser of that realm. He walked in the God-realm—the realm of faith. This made him righteous.

You see, from the life of Abraham, we can learn so many insights. He pioneered the movement of faith and we can look at him and learn the concept of faith. Irrespective of what he was dealing with, he knew the merits of walking with God. Abraham knew that to walk with God is to be in the majority. Hence, he counted himself in the army of God. Being on the Lord's side is the greatest advantage. This is what I want you to learn—to keep walking with God.

You might be reading this and you are dealing with so much now, but I want you to keep walking with God. Situations change, but God doesn't. God changes situations. He did for Abraham. Abraham had his situation turn around and so did other people throughout the scriptures. As I take you through this book, I would bring you to people who walked with God and the rewards they attained. Irrespective of the circumstances they were dealing with, they rather chose to follow and honor God. In the end, God honored them as well. This makes us see that faith is currency and can be rewarded.

Personally, I have seen God reward me in many ways. As of the time of this writing, I am entering my eighth decade in life, and following after God has brought me so much reward. God has graciously been there for me even in the darkest seasons of life. It is this faith in God that has sustained me. I look around and I cannot see most of the people I grew up with and they are dead or in some miserable place of life. But Jesus in my case has turned that to joyful seasons. He has shown me great mercy and life-eternal. What has birthed that glory is very simple—walking with God. God is very faithful when it comes to all those who honor and serve Him well. In my case, He has proven His faithfulness many times. Even in a strange land, God has prospered me and showed me great mercy.

Friend, as you glean through these pages, I want you to know that you have to keep your faith in God. That is the greatest thing to do— following after God. When you come to the face of challenges, keep walking with God. When the economy is in recession, keep walking with God. When the marriage is shaking and things are falling apart, keep walking with God. When you are believing to make it into college and there are no funds to sponsor that, keep walking with God. When you are in the fixes and there seems to be no way, keep walking with God. It is in the walking with God that there are great rewards. Let this challenge you to keep your eyes focused on the Lord and nothing else.

Most times when we are going through challenges, instead of focusing on God, we are focusing on the challenges instead. This is wrong! Every challenge before the Lord is nothing He can change all things in a split second. Luke 1:37 asserted that with God all things are possible. So, we have to believe in the power of God that makes all things possible. This faith keeps us in the darkness and pushes us to rise above those circumstances.

What I want to bring to you through this book is a stirring into faith. I want you to come with me as we delve into this for greater impact.

CHAPTER ONE

GOD REWARDS FAITH

Faith is a divine essence. A slight demonstration of it attracts heavens resources. And above all, the inherent glory within is unleashed."

Edward Djamome

God is a God who honors faith. Wherever faith is demonstrated, God honors it. What moves God is faith. Every supernatural transaction is predicated on faith. Faith is the very core of divine transactions. Anyone who gains this understanding will be able to achieve greater things with God. Without it, it is impossible to please God.

Remember what Paul asserted. Paul mentioned that faith is what pleases God. In his letter to the church, he named that without faith, no one can please God (See Hebrews 11:6). This should make us understand the power of faith. Many are deceived thinking these things move God. On the contrary, these don't move God at all. Faith is what God is interested in. What moves God is not money, fame, title, or cars, but faith. Wherever faith is demonstrated, God is interested. I will begin to take you into events so you can see the power of faith how God intervened in people's circumstances because of the faith they demonstrated. This should encourage us to walk in faith.

We can never talk about faith without talking about Abraham. He is the first man to demonstrate faith in its fullness. He believed in God and that caused God to call him His friend. The moment faith is seen, God is interested. You see, many of us when we are confronted with the challenges of life, we lose our faith alongside. But that should never be the case. Challenges are meant to strengthen our faith so we can walk with God. We are supposed to keep walking with God. That is how we can be able to experience the realities of God—these dimensions are only experienced in faith.

Let's come to take a vivid look at the life of Abraham. You come to know that Abraham was born to Terah and he was an idol worshiper. In the place where he grew up, they worshipped idols. However, Abraham grew up loving God and seeking the Lord. It was this pursuit that made God discover him. The moment God discovered this man, Abraham, He promised him that He was going to bless him in all he was doing. Let's look at the wording here:

"Now the Lord had said unto Abram, Get thee out of thy country, and from thy kindred, and from thy father's house, unto a land that I will shew thee: And I will make of thee a great nation, and I will bless thee, and make thy name great; and thou shalt be a blessing: And I will bless them that bless thee, and curse him that curseth thee: and in thee shall all families of the earth be blessed."—(Genesis 12:1—3)

This season he, Abraham, hadn't left his father. God appeared and began to commune with him. God asked that he leaves his father and mother and go to a land that He God was going to show him. His obedience was going to result in him accessing the blessing of God. The promise was that he was going to become a great nation. And anyone who blesses him is going to be blessed and anyone who curses him was going to be cursed as well. What great assurance to come from the mouth of God! All of us have to secure similar truths from the Lord. This will change everything around us. Glory!

Understand here that these words didn't come from a prophet but the Lord. The Lord spoke these words at the expense of His integrity. He knew He was going to perform the words that He had said. So, He said it with all confidence. If there was going to be a delay, it wasn't because He was not able to do it, but because Abraham didn't believe Him.

With all these promises, Abraham still didn't have a child. However, He didn't give up walking with God. He continued to walk with God even though there were things he needed from God which were not granted yet. In his mind, he had concluded that he was never going to have a child. However, God had something else in mind. God started communicating about blessing him and increasing him to be a great nation, Abraham brought this issue up again.

Genesis 15 unravels this very issue. He asked God, saying, "what would you give me seeing I go childless? This is telling you that Abraham was reasoning as a normal man here. He had not yet caught the revelation of what God promised him. God had to push him to that place of absolute faith. The moment he got that faith activated, then he talked differently. You see, when your faith level is down, it becomes very difficult to believe all that God is intended to do. This was what was happening to Abraham here. He was staggering in faith here.

"After these things the word of the Lord came unto Abram in a vision, saying, Fear not, Abram: I [am] thy shield, [and] thy exceeding great reward. And Abram said, Lord God, what wilt thou give me, seeing I go childless, and the steward of my house [is] this Eliezer of Damascus? And Abram said, Behold, to me thou hast given no seed: and, lo, one born in my house is mine heir."—(Genesis 15:1—3)

He had not yet come to have his faith activated. At this point, you can see his communication was different. This tells us that Abraham was speaking on the human plain. Which was still normal because he was dealing with a challenge. What God did to remedy the situation was that he had to give him an experience that would lift his faith up. Seeing he was lagging in faith, God asked him to come out of the tent. He did come and out and was asked to lift his eyes and count the stars in the heavens. All this had a purpose—to stir him to faith.

"And he brought him forth abroad, and said, Look now toward heaven, and tell the stars, if thou be able to number them: and he said unto him, So shall thy seed be. And he believed in the Lord; and he counted it to him for righteousness."—(Genesis 15:5—6)

Do you see that? God made him count the stars. He possibly started to count and lost figures. Then his faith popped open and he was able to see what God was seeing. From that experience, Abraham's faith changed and he learned to take God at His word. This is how Abraham gained stature with God.

When God asked him to leave his family from this point, he went out looking for that city that the builder of that city was God. He knew the merits that came alongside that obedience. Indeed, he found the city. How? Through faith. Faith is what he used to access this very promise.

Now here is the question, how long did it take before this very promise came pass? It took twenty-five years before this promise came to pass. This was not a prophet that spoke the words, but the Lord gave that word, but it took twenty-five years to manifest. However, Abraham didn't stop walking with God. He kept walking with God knowing that the One who promised him was able to deliver.

Are you persuaded that the one who promised you can deliver His promise? Abraham was fully persuaded. He believed that God was able to deliver that which He had promised. Romans 4:21 asserts that Abraham was convinced beyond every reasonable doubt that God was able to perform His promise. This motivated him to keep walking with God. There were days he felt like giving up, but he didn't dare do that. There were days in his pursuit he felt like he couldn't make it anymore, but he believed and went toward the promise. Against all hope, he moved towards the promise in strong faith.

"(As it is written, I have made thee a father of many nations,) before him whom he believed, [even] God, who quickeneth the dead, and calleth those things which be not as though they were. Who against hope believed in hope, that he might become the father of many nations; according to that which was spoken, So shall thy seed be. And being not weak in faith, he considered not his own body now dead, when he was about an hundred years old, neither yet the deadness of Sara's womb: He staggered not at the promise of God through unbelief; but was strong in faith, giving glory to God; And being fully persuaded that, what he had promised, he was able also to perform."— (Romans 4:17—21)

God's dealing with this gentleman, Abraham was outstanding. Even though He wasn't ready to do it yet, but He wanted him to believe in His ability. God wanted to cause the shift in his mental conditioning before He could have that real experience. The moment Abraham had this shift, God, therefore, called the things which are not as though they were. Abraham therefore believed and then he went towards the promise of God, not in unbelief, but strong faith giving glory to God.

He moved against all doubts and then he was praising God in great faith. That is how we all have to approach life. We have to approach life and God in faith. The goal of all things is to walk in the fullness of faith knowing that He who has begun the good work is able to bring that work to an end. We are to know that God who called us out of darkness is able to do exceedingly and abundantly above all things. This understanding helps so much to survive even the greatest ordeals of life. Abraham could have faced so much pain, names, and attacks as well, however, he kept walking with God because he was fully persuaded.

When a man is fully convinced by the divine, there is nothing that can shake the man. He can stand and fight through the greatest odds of life. Abraham for example had the greatest test of all, but he never shook in faith. He kept walking. Were there days he felt like giving up? Too many times. Were they days he felt God was never going to come through for Him? Surely! Did he give up? No way! If he did, he was never going to inherit the promises that he did inherit. The reason he did was because of the faith that he had in God.

You see, in life, there are challenges that are presented before us each day. We are all going to be tested in one way or the other. We will be given promises that might linger on the way. In those times, what are you going to do? Would you dare believe God like that of Abraham? Or you are going to give up? What are you going to do when everything you have believed in is failing or falling away? What would you do in the darkness where you are stroking and seeking light and there is none? That is the same place Abraham found himself for twenty-five years. Before Isaac came, he had to walk through those lands of loneliness and doubts altogether. However, he went through that believing in God. He knew that God was able to deliver His promises to Him.

You as well have to learn from this so that it can encourage your walk with the Lord. Where there is faith, there is always a reward. Abraham's faith was rewarded. This tells us that God rewards faith. Anyone who dares walk in faith is never going to be left unattended to by God.

Jacob's Example Of Faith

Another man we can look at is Jacob. He is an example of faith. He understood this concept of walking with God. This is what saved him and repositioned him. We all know the life of Jacob and how cunning he was. He knew the mystery of negotiations. Jacob negotiated everything. When his brother, Esau came to him asking if he could help him with food, he negotiated and got his birthright. And another time, Jacob fought his way into receiving the blessing that was meant for Esau. This was who he was—a cunning man. However, he was also a lover of God.

After taking his brother's birthright, he was running away and he got to Bethel. He was seeking refuge from the wrath of his brother. This was what triggered his encounter with the Lord. You see, sometimes the things that happen to us often lead us to our very possible selves. In other words, the disadvantage often is leading us to the advantage. He was running away only to run into his purpose. From that encounter, his perspective about life changed.

"And Esau hated Jacob because of the blessing wherewith his father blessed him: and Esau said in his heart, The days of mourning for my father are at hand; then will I slay my brother Jacob. And these words of Esau her elder son were told to Rebekah: and she sent and called Jacob her younger son, and said unto him, Behold, thy brother Esau, as touching thee, doth comfort himself, [purposing] to kill thee. Now therefore, my son, obey my voice; and arise, flee thou to Laban my brother to Haran; And tarry with him a few days, until thy brother's fury turn away; Until thy brother's anger turn away from thee, and he forget [that] which thou hast done to him: then I will send, and fetch thee from thence: why should I be deprived also of you both in one day?"— (Genesis 27:41—45)

After this encounter, Rebekah encouraged Jacob to run to Laban. The reason was that Esau was very angry and had purposed in his heart that the moment his father dies, he was going to kill Jacob to compensate for his anger. Understand something here, killing Jacob was never going to undo what was done. So, you must never make that mistake. Killing the people who offended you cannot undo what they have done. Each one of us must learn to carry a forgiving heart. That is how we can change things.

Esau was overtaken by that action. This made him make that decision. However the information got to Rebekah no one knows. But she strictly sent Jacob away. As he was running away, he was running into God. He had left family, but God was now beginning to take responsibility for his life. His heart was been worked upon. He used that opportunity to reveal certain dimensions of Himself to Jacob. Jacob's encounter on the stone that revealed heaven and the angels was God's way of getting into his heart so he could focus on Him.

"And Jacob went out from Beer–sheba, and went toward Haran. And he lighted upon a certain place, and tarried there all night, because the sun was set; and he took of the stones of that place, and put [them for] his pillows, and lay down in that place to sleep. And he dreamed, and behold a ladder set up on the earth, and the top of it reached to heaven: and behold the angels of God ascending and descending on it. And, behold, the Lord stood above it, and said, I [am] the Lord God of Abraham thy father, and the God of Isaac: the land whereon thou liest, to thee will I give it, and to thy seed; And thy seed shall be as the dust of the earth, and thou shalt spread abroad to the west, and to the east, and to the north, and to the south: and in thee and in thy seed shall all the families of the earth be blessed. And, behold, I [am] with thee, and

will keep thee in all [places] whither thou goest, and will bring thee again into this land; for I will not leave thee, until I have done [that] which I have spoken to thee of. And Jacob awaked out of his sleep, and he said, Surely the Lord is in this place; and I knew [it] not. "—(Genesis 28:10—16)

God used this encounter to get into his heart to break him down. The way Jacob was wired, it was going to be very difficult for him to walk in faith. Hence, there was a need for a divine orchestration to lead him to great faith. God did this very thing to bring him to that place of faith. This awakening was what was going to reposition him so God could execute His purposes in his life. Seeing this very encounter, you can see that his communication changed. The moment he knew that God was there and God was for him, he changed his way of talking and faith came alive within his spirit. This was the same faith he used to prosper in the house of Laban. Laban was the type of boss who didn't want his subordinates to prosper. However, with grace, Jacob overcame all that. He succeeded in all that he was doing.

When the grace of God is at work in your life, it doesn't matter who is unhappy with you. You are going to excel in all things—this is the promise of God to all who are saved—that we all may excel in all things. The evidence is very clear in the life of Jacob. By the time he came out of Laban's house, he was fully blessed and enlarged. He entered there broke and poor, but he came out a blessed man strong as a nation. What happened to him? He discovered the God factor. The God-factor was what ushered him into the new realms of life.

This is what we all have to learn from. We have to learn how to walk with God in faith knowing that every invested faith has a reward attached to it. No one walks in faith that is not going to be

19

rewarded. Jacob who walked in faith was rewarded. His faith each day was recorded in heaven and in due time, God rewarded him. This should make you understand that God rewards faith. When we believe, He rewards it.

We can see that Jacob believed the Lord. He kept his covenant with God even in adverse conditions. When he got to Laban's place, he was maltreating him. However, he didn't give up on his God. He rather was getting closer to God in fellowship. He developed his relationship with God in negative circumstances. We have to equally do the same. Negativity should never stop us from growing our faith and developing our relationships with God. The more we discover that our relationship with God is an integral part of becoming what He has promised us, then we will do everything possible to make that happen.

God is not a man. He cannot lie. Whatever is ever promised, we can count on it because the One who promised is able to make it happen, that is, come to pass. We have to dare believe Him. No circumstances should make us doubt God. We will be doing ourselves and God disservice when we walk in unbelief. The way to accessing divine treasures and realities is in the place of faith. God, Himself, desires to bring each one of us to the place of experience in life, however, the way to that experience is faith. Faith is what is going to make that happen. Without faith, no one can be rewarded with that experience.

We see Jacob realizing that if he was going to have an experience with divine protection, provision, and fellowship, he needed to keep walking with God. That understanding made him form his alliance with the Lord very quickly. He had come out of the place of safety to a place where he was uncertain of the safety and this time he knew that he had to believe in the Lord. As he threw his faith to God, God rewarded him. You as well, if you learn this concept of faith, you will be intrigued and amazed at what God is going to do with your life. God rewards every faith that is invested. Understand that what God works with is faith. Faith is the medium of exchange for God. Therefore, we have to learn this.

The reward of Jacob was so great. He went in empty but came out a blessed man. That means God rewards faith. Anyone who forms an alliance with God in faith is always divinely met and assisted. So, this is your challenge today to walk in faith knowing that God rewards faith.

The Woman With The Issue Of Blood's Example

Another clear example we can learn the concept of faith and how it was rewarded is the woman with the issue of blood. This very woman is nameless in the Bible. The Bible concealed her name for whatever reason. But her faith in God in the midst of her situation is beyond words. It is very clear that it took great faith for her to get the kind of miracle that she got. When she got to the end of herself and her efforts, she knew that it was only God who could change the situation. What she did was that she purposed in her heart that if she can but touch the hem of Jesus' garment, she was going to be whole. Indeed, as she believed, God did it.

"And a certain woman, which had an issue of blood twelve years, And had suffered many things of many physicians, and had spent all that she had, and was nothing bettered, but rather grew worse, When she had heard of Jesus, came in the press behind, and touched his garment. For she said, If I may touch but his clothes, I shall be whole. And straightway the fountain of her blood was dried up; and she felt in [her] body that she was healed of that plague. And Jesus, immediately knowing in himself that virtue had

gone out of him, turned him about in the press, and said, Who touched my clothes? And his disciples said unto him, Thou seest the multitude thronging thee, and sayest thou, Who touched me? And he looked round about to see her that had done this thing. But the woman fearing and trembling, knowing what was done in her, came and fell down before him, and told him all the truth. And he said unto her, Daughter, thy faith hath made thee whole; go in peace, and be whole of thy plague."—(Mark 5:25—34)

Reading through this account is so overwhelming. You will definitely get teary reading the ordeal of this very woman. She suffered this hemorrhage not for one week, but for twelve years. The record indicates that in her time, there was no hospital or physician she had not visited. She reached out to every place where there were rumors of help. And interestingly, none of those people could help her. Everything she tried, she only exhausted herself and all that she had.

The situation got bad and bad each day to a point that she was left with nothing—she was drained financially. That means there was no hope for her to remedy the situation again. How was she going to take care of the hospital bills if she visited the hospital? She stayed at home and wishing to die. Do you know that situation where the doctors give up on you? That is what happened to this woman. She went home and was now ready to draw her curtains amongst the living. Even if she was ready to live, but the stigma for living was beyond words. You will notice that at this time, Jesus had not yet died, and hence the law was still in effect. And under the law, when a woman is going through her menstruations, she was named unclean. This woman was named "unclean" for this twelve years. She had to walk through the streets having fingers pointed at her.

Just imagine how she was going to go about this whole thing. She was dealing with pain, and then people were as well a pain she had to deal with. Because there is no way she was not going to have people talking about her. It went on and on until it was noised abroad a certain day that Jesus was coming into town. This noise about Jesus was different. Because the reports she heard possibly suggested, "This Jesus doesn't turn away people irrespective of who you are."

With this mindset of wanting love, peace, and joy again, she purposed in her heart that if she can but touch Jesus, she was going to be well no matter what. In her heart, she was so convinced that she was going to get better. And as famous as Jesus was in that day, as He walked on the dusty streets, many people were thronging on Him. This woman passed through the press and touched the hem of Jesus' garments and indeed, as she had purposed in her heart, it was done for her. Glory! That is the power of faith, friend! Faith brings to manifestation that which man cannot do.

After that touch, power went out of Jesus. She turned to His right-hand men and asked them, "Who touched me?" Peter who was outspoken of them all began to talk and said that "Lord, you can see that people are many here and you are asking, who touched me?" Peter didn't know it was a touch that had to do with the transmission of virtue and power. Jesus went further to explain what happened there. This woman now fearing and knowing that Jesus had an awareness of what happened came forward and fell before Jesus.

What outstands me is the response of Jesus after hearing the woman's pain. Jesus didn't judge her in any way. Jesus brought her into that place to experience what she never got out there—love. For the first time, she heard someone make time for her and talk to her with that kind of passion, and connection. She was looking at the face of Jesus as seeing the shades and flashes of love. That broke the shackles of her affliction and warmed her up in love as well. She got into the presence of Jesus seeking a miracle but leaves the presence of Jesus with a relationship. This is telling us what Jesus is able to reach out to make of the very desires in our hearts.

You might be asking, "Pastor Lola, how is that happening?" Jesus' response to this woman brings us to that understanding. Jesus said to her, "Daughter, thy faith hath made thee whole; go in peace, and be whole of thy plague." Understand here that Jesus didn't say, "Daughter, My power has made you whole." He rather said, "Your faith." That is telling us that the woman had the answer to what she was looking for within her, but she didn't know how to harness the answers. She wasn't taught how to use that faith she was having to gain answers from God. This is what is happening to many children of God today as well. They are carrying within the faith, but they don't know how to use that faith to access the creative realm of God.

This woman at this point understood this dimension. The moment she used it, God reached out to her and ended her affliction. Her twelve years' affliction ended and she stepped into a new season of her life. This can equally happen to you as well.   You can get divinely attended to if you can dare believe God for your restoration and increase. God is ever ready to reach out to you and change things around you, however, you need faith.

Faith is the very element that links God's creative power to your circumstances. Without faith, nothing is ever going to happen. That dimension of God is only concealed until faith is produced. The manifestation of faith is the manifestation of that realm. When God sees that faith, then He activates that realm of power and creativity. My goal in writing this book to you is to make you understand that

God rewards faith. Every demonstration of faith is ever going to be rewarded by God. God rewards faith.

When we learn to walk with God in faith and not look at the circumstances we are dealing with, there are going to be changes in all things. You will notice that the woman shifted her attention from what she was dealing with and now began to focus on something else—the Lord. The moment she did that, she created a platform for a divine transaction to happen. That was the beginning of divine assistance in her life.

Personally, I have seen God come into my life and helped me in many ways. As of the time of this writing, I am entering my eighth decade and I am a great grandmother. I have seen a few things in this life. God has come in many ways to help me and my family out of the cares of this world. Through this journey—life, I have come to understand that anyone who dares to put his or her trust on the Lord is never kept to shame. The Lord helps everyone who believes. There is no one that is ever going to be kept to shame. That has never happened.

There had been days in my life where it looked like it was never going to be possible to make it, but God showed but. When I look at the New Glory International Ministries where it is planted, I can see nothing but the hand of the Lord. From a strange land, God has established me in the United Kingdom. He by His sovereign power and grace has shown me great ability. He has established and increased me in many ways. This is how I know that if you can place your faith in God, He is never going to fail you in any way. He has divinely supplied my needs and wants. He has also healed my body in many ways that space wouldn't allow me to write about.

When I even look around and see that many of the people I started life with are not even in existence, then I know that God has a purpose for my life as a whole. He sustained me for the remnant of the Commonwealth of Israel. Thus, that men might be redirected to purpose and God as well. That is what I have been doing all the time of the manifestation of the New Glory International Ministries—helping men love God more and more.

I can boldly say, it doesn't matter your circumstances, if you can believe God, He is going to usher you into new dimensions of life. You are going to be stunned at how far God can take you and your family if you ever dare to trust Him. He has never and will never fail anyone. From the three stories you read, you will notice that He has not failed any of them—not even during the times of the delays. What I am beckoning on you now is to embrace faith knowing that God is never going to fail you. Keep walking in faith.

Circumstances might force you to think God is going to fail you, but don't get perturbed. He is never going to fail you. God is ever ready to reach out to you. However, you must be willing to give Him your hand to help you out. That process is what I call faith. Trusting that giving your heart will result in divine assistance. Having this assurance that God is ever going to come through for His people, you should learn to walk in faith. In the next chapter, I will encourage you to believe in God. I will encourage you to believe in God regardless of what you are dealing with in life. Your circumstances can never shake God out of the throne. Hence, you need to believe Him and take Him at His word. What He said He is going to do, He is going to do no matter what.

CHAPTER TWO

LEARN THE CONCEPT OF FAITH

"Unshakable faith shakes up everything!"—Jonathan Nettles

The concept of faith is what encompasses the worship of God. Without faith, there is nothing that comes from the spirit realm. God is a spirit and it has to take faith to relate with a spirit. And this concept we have to learn it—that is, learning to believe in the Lord. From the first chapter, we understood that God rewards faith. Now what is expected of us is that we have to learn that concept so that the reward of faith can be made manifest.

There are many people in the world today who are wondering how they can get faith and walk in faith. In as much as they love God, they find themselves in the circumstances of life where there is a need for faith to be used and therein you find them in confusion. Questions like, "Do I really believe?" and if I do, "Why are my situations not changing?" These are questions many people have asked. Sometimes even the clergy. You see, faith in as much as it is one of the greatest forces that govern the earth, it is always going to be subjected to a test. This explains why challenges come on our way. Most times challenges are platforms for us to grow our faith and discover the inherent glories that come with faith.

Faith is a force that governs the universe. God created the universe to work by this "faith principle" and without it, productivity is not possible. It will surprise you that everyone in this world is walking in faith in the world. Understand that there are dimensions of faith. Faith is in levels, from weak faith to strong faith. That explains that everyone in this world has faith. Let me give you an example, reading this book, you possibly could be sitting on a chair or lying on your bed. You had faith that the chair was going to hold you and that is why you sat on it. What you did was that you placed faith on the chair that it was not going to break but to be able to hold you. That is faith. It is called weak faith. Just that it cannot get you into the creative dimension of the supernatural.

And from this, we have little faith. This faith can produce miracles. Jesus asserted that if we have this as small as a mustard seed, we can move mountains. Do you understand the power in it? This means that if we translate this little faith into a spiritual context, we can achieve marvelous things. Let's look at His assertions:

"Then Jesus answered and said, O faithless and perverse generation, how long shall I be with you? how long shall I suffer you? bring him hither to me. And Jesus rebuked the devil; and he departed out of him: and the child was cured from that very hour. Then came the disciples to Jesus apart, and said, Why could not we cast him out? And Jesus said unto them, Because of your unbelief: for verily I say unto you, If ye have faith as a grain of mustard seed, ye shall say unto this mountain, Remove hence to yonder place; and it shall remove; and nothing shall be impossible unto you."—(Mathew 17:17—20)

Before Jesus made these awesome and insightful truths, He had taken some of the disciples to the mountain top to have an experience that could make them understand the full scope of His assignment. It was on this mountain that Moses and Elijah appeared and the disciples heard the audible voice of God. While He was there with James, Peter, and John, the others were at the base of the mountain. Whatever they were doing, nothing much was recorded. In the process, we find this gentleman who had a son who was suffering from a lunatic spirit. This spirit will often cast him into water or fire. This man brought his son to the disciples and they tried and they couldn't cast out the devil.

When Jesus heard that they couldn't cast out the devil, He got disappointed and then addressed the issue. Look at where He started from—their faith. He expressed His displeasure and then registered into their spirit that it was a faith problem. Then He rebuked the devil. Then He taught them the glory that faith carries. Every faith has inherent energies and vibrations in it. The moment we learn how to harness that; we can access the creative dimension of God's power. That is to say, we can get God working in and through anything.

You see, faith is the center of life. Without it, it will be difficult to get things done. So, do you see how important faith is? Jesus made it very clear that with it, we can move mountains. These mountains He was addressing here were talking about the circumstances of life. He was addressing the issues and the ordeals we face each day. They are mountains. The way to get them out of the way is through faith. Faith makes things possible.

And then we have strong faith. This dimension of faith comes as you continue to use your faith. As you use your faith, it grows and grows. Do you know that faith has life in it? Because it can grow. Whatever is a living organism ought to grow. Faith is a living organism and therefore it grows. This is why we are told to grow our faith from whatever level it is so it can become great and strong faith. Abraham got to this dimension.

When we read the account in Romans 4 about the life of Abraham, we could see that when the promise of God was given to him concerning Isaac, he moved towards that promise against all nature and reality not in unbelief, but in strong faith giving glory to God. Paul's assertion is nothing but reality. No wonder God called Abraham His friend. Faith is what interests God. I registered this at the beginning of the book that wherever faith is demonstrated, God is there. What attracts God is faith. For anyone who wants to walk in an atmosphere that is saturated with the glory and power of God, then faith has to come in. It is very essential to understand this very concept.

You be reading this and you might be asking, "Pastor Lola, how can one get faith and how can one increase in faith?" Great thought. Faith, remember, comes from hearing the Word of God. The Word of God is what faith feeds on to grow. The life of faith is in the Word of God. In other words, what makes faith productive and efficient is the Word of God.

"How then shall they call on him in whom they have not believed? and how shall they believe in him of whom they have not heard? and how shall they hear without a preacher? And how shall they preach, except they be sent? as it is written, How beautiful are the feet of them that preach the gospel of peace, and bring glad tidings of good things! But they have not all obeyed the gospel. For Esaias saith, Lord, who hath believed our report? So then faith [cometh] by hearing, and hearing by the word of God."—(Romans 10:14—17)

Look at the assertion of Paul here. He made it very clear that for one to believe, there has to be a preacher. I agree with Paul. The preacher there is the one who communicates the Word of God. The Word must be conveyed to a person or the audience and the way to go about that is there has to be a preacher. And before one can fulfill that duty, he or she must be called to do that. The result of that preaching is that it ignites faith. preaching the Word of God ignites faith.

In that very text, Paul outlined how faith gains access to the human spirit—preaching. Just as I mentioned. Hearing the Word of God through preaching is what brings faith. Faith comes through hearing the Word of God. And that is communicated through preaching. So, we understand that faith comes through hearing the Word of God, and the way to sustain that is through the continuous hearing of the Word of God. If you look at the woman with the issue of blood, it

31

was the reports she heard about Jesus that enacted her faith. She had heard that Jesus had the power to heal and was ever welcoming. Therefore, she leaped that message to have an experience and the result was that her faith was rewarded.

Friend, you need to understand this concept of faith. It will help you for life. This is how you can be able to create possibilities for yourself in your way with God. Understand that without faith, no one can get anything from God. This is the simple rule!

Faith Is A Necessity Of Life

Faith is a necessity in life. Without it, no one can receive anything from God. It is as simple as that. God can never get involved in something that there is no faith in. So, anyone who wants to do business with God, such one must learn this concept of faith and walk in it. It is very key and elementary as well.

"Now faith is the substance of things hoped for, the evidence of things not seen. For by it the elders obtained a good report. Through faith we understand that the worlds were framed by the word of God, so that things which are seen were not made of things which do appear. By faith Abel offered unto God a more excellent sacrifice than Cain, by which he obtained witness that he was righteous, God testifying of his gifts: and by it he being dead yet speaketh. By faith Enoch was translated that he should not see death; and was not found, because God had translated him: for before his translation he had this testimony, that he pleased God. But without faith [it is] impossible to please [him]: for he that cometh to God must believe that he is, and [that] he is a rewarder of them that diligently seek him. "—(Hebrews 11:1—6)

Understand something here; God allowed us to see the merit that came with faith. What happened here is that faith will always be rewarded as I mentioned to you in chapter one. The elders here obtained a good report through faith. The reward entirely was quantified as a good report. And this is the greatest legacy in life—that is, having God speak good about you. That is priceless!

Now later, we can see another concept there as well. We can see that faith is what made the world stand today. God created all things, and He did that on the principle of faith. Faith is what God used to create the world and the things that are in it. So, we can see that the world is hanging on the balance of faith. Everything is ruled and governed by the principle of faith. This is why if there is anything we can spend our lives developing and growing, it should be our faith. Faith is very essential and it is the necessity of life. Learning the concept means we are preparing ourselves to walk in the glory it comes with.

This is the same principle Abel and Enoch walked in. We understand Enoch walked with faith to a point that he didn't want to die and God had to translate him. That is where his faith could reach. And then God allowed it to be recorded that without faith, no one can please God. That means that anything happening outside the faith, God is not interested. What captures God's attention more is faith. This is what Enoch understood. The record is very clear that before his translation, he had a testimony that he walked with God and God was happy with him. What a great testimony to be written about you! We have to learn this principle so that when we carry great testimonies when the chronicles of the kings are read.

Faith is what you need in life. Even if you are going into business, the first capital you need is not money, but faith. Faith is substance and capital. The next time you are asked whether you have the capital for that business, you have to respond as a person of faith. The reason is: You have the first capital which is faith. It is the best capital at that matter. There is no storm or business decrease that can shake this capital. No matter how the market goes, this "capital" will always be intact. Learn this and you will be stunned how productive you can become.

Learn Faith—That Is Where The Future Is Created

We have to understand something here; that faith creates things. The future is in faith and the way to create that is through faith. I will show you that you can create your world of possibilities with faith. How did Abraham translate that glory from the spiritual realm into the physical realm, faith? Faith is the very element that was used. This explains why he was called the father of faith. The reason? He always practiced and walked in faith. His life was and is an example of faith.

Abraham, for example, believed in God for everything. The moment God knew that Abraham gave Him the opportunity to be responsible, God demonstrated that. Faith is granting God the opportunity to be "responsible." When this is understood, God will be given access into your life without any delay. Because you help Him to help you create a world of unlimited possibilities.

The purpose of this book is to bring you to the place of full faith in God irrespective of the circumstances of life. I am entering my eighth decade in life and trust me, I have come to understand that the greatest place to invest life is in God and the safest place in life is in God. Anyone who wants to make an impact and live long as well must learn to believe in God.

So, be encouraged to learn the concept of faith in God. The thing is this; the world system is falling every day. And we have to learn the concept of faith for survival. The truth of the matter is this: Your safety and well-being are not in any government. They come with many promises each day and get you to think they are there for you, but the reality is this, they are there for themselves. Therefore, you have to understand this and believe in God for life. When you believe, then you are creating a future that no government has power over.

The moment your life is supplied by the government, then they have power over everything. But when your life is from heaven and God, no government can shake the future that is created. Understand that Abraham's legacy can never be erased or terminated. Why? He didn't have faith in a government, but God. He believed in God and God is bigger than any government. The moment you believe your life around the government, as long as there is government rotation and economic recessions, you are not safe. You see that you will go to bed and you are not sleeping because you don't know what is going to happen the next second. In other words, there is no safety.

It is therefore wise to know that the surest way to create the future is through the fundamental principle of life—faith. The future of safety, health, and prosperity is created on faith. Truth be told, it is what you need for life. Gaining this insight can change your whole scope of life. Trust me.

Faith Never Disappoints

This is the reason why you need to learn the concept of faith. Faith never disappoints. The reason is that faith is one of the things that is going to abide forever. In Paul's letter to the church in Corinth, he mentioned that three things are going to abide forever, which are, faith, hope, and love (See 1 Corinthians 13:13). There is life in faith and that life is eternal. That means when we put that to work, everything that evolves around it is as well eternal.

God produced faith and provided what is going to keep it alive as well—that is, the Word of God. The Word is the atmosphere in which faith can thrive. God, Himself is eternal. So, walking in faith, means that we are dealing with an eternal system. Therefore, whatever we are using it for, there is lasting power in that thing that is established on the foundation of faith.

Faith is very essential and we need it in our walk with God. Without it, no one as Hebrews 11:6 asserted, can please God. The way to please God and glorify God is through faith. We have to be encouraged to walk in it because it is never going to fail. Faith never disappoints. There is no one who has ever walked with God and God has failed him. When it comes to that point where God didn't come through, then the problem came from the person and not God.

When Abraham believed God for Isaac, he had Isaac. When Abraham believed God to become the father of many nations, he became the father of many nations. When Jacob believed God for Him to take him to Laban's house and bring him back safely, he got that granted. When blind Bartimaeus believed God for the restoration of his sight, he got that granted. When Joseph believed God in a strange land, God kept him and made him a prime minister in the land. When the woman with the issue of blood believed Jesus for healing, she got that answered.

Everyone who ever placed faith in God was never disappointed. God came through for the person. From believing God for bread to raising the dead. Each occurrence of faith, God stepped in— including situations that were at the detriment of the people's life.

For example, when we look at the three Hebrew boys, how God recused them from the fire in Daniel three. We can see that God is ever faithful and He cannot fail. Therefore, it will be unwise to throw down our faith. We should rather keep it up knowing that God is going to come through for us.

God has never failed anyone. This nature is something we can count on and He is never going to change. He is the same yesterday, today, and forever (See Hebrews 13:8). That means that we can count on Him when He gives us a promise. We can hold Him at His word and He is never going to disappoint. The God in whom we believe doesn't disappoint and just as faith.

Learn From The Example Of Others

The way to secure motivation is through the example of others. Watching others achieve their promises and results is a priceless feeling. What that communicates are the possibilities that are made available in life. Knowing that what God did for someone, can be done, is reviving. Friend, understand that what God can do for one, He can do for all. This revelation can bring new hope amidst darkness and hardness.

What helped me come this far is the confidence in God and His ability. Reading through the stories of how God has helped people through the scriptures, I know that it is God's duty and responsibility to help me as well to reach my maximum potential. He has helped me so much in this life and now that I am entering eighty, I can confidently say that God never fails. There has never been a season in life that He has failed me. What built my faith is coming to know that what He has done for one, He can do for all. I read how God helped Jacob prospered in strange lands. Then that became my motivation. In the U.K where I am now as at the time of this writing,

God has helped me. I have a Nigerian root, but God has established me in the land and ushered me before the princes of the land.

New Glory International Ministries is rooted in the United Kingdom and God has helped us in every step of the way. Right from our inception until now, God has been so faithful to us. This has always thrilled me and challenged me in every way. Knowing that God who sustains and provides is always there is such an amazing understanding. Indeed, I and the children that God has given me are for signs and for wonders. How did we arrive here? Faith. Jacob left home and fugitive but came back established with substance after an encounter. The glory of life is birthed as a result of encounters. It was an encounter with God that changed all things.

When I look at the New Glory International Ministries, from the one person to the hundreds, God has been so amazing. I know it is nothing but the hand of God. That is the product of my faith in God. This faith has paid off. This makes me encourage you. I write this book just to bring you that encouragement as well to keep your faith in God. Irrespective of what you are doing now, learn to believe in God. Because faith is an asset of investment that will pay off in this life.

A believing man can survive against all. Before someone dies, what they lose is faith and the strength to survive. The moment they lose that; the body gives up. This assertion I am making is the will to stay. This is why when someone is dying, you hear people saying, "Just hold on…fight on." Why are they saying that? They are saying that to keep the faith of the person alive. A believing man will outlive his pain. Hallelujah!

Jacob outlived his pain. The woman with the issue of blood outlived her pain. Abraham outlived his pain. Joseph outlived his pain. The children of Israel outlived their pain. Joshua outlived his pain. And many others who dared to believe God. Faith always rewards. They believed and lived longer than what they were going through. This means that if we can as well believe in God, we can live longer than what we are dealing with. The insight is this; the life within the circumstance is shorter than ours. So, we don't have to look at the challenges but focus on developing ourselves for a better future.

Be encouraged with the stories in the Bible about how people believed in God. God allowed those stories to be written for our learning and comfort. We are even encouraged to follow those who through faith obtained the promise. Therefore, we have to learn from others who walked with God and saw the merits. This will encourage us in our walk with God as well.

The goal is to keep companionship with God no matter what we are dealing with. The place to drive motivation is in the Word of God where it has been outlined a few examples of people who walked with God and saw His merits and power. So, be encouraged as well to follow the example of faith will always pay and we have to learn the concept of faith.

Faith Will Always Pay Off

Faith is currency. Where there is currency, there can be transactions done. We can see that anytime you have money and you go into the market, you can buy things. That is something that has to do with faith. The moment faith is in place; it can do transactions in the spirit. When we are walking with God, we have to learn to believe in Him. The reason is that our faith will enable the transaction of what God has to offer us.

When we look at Abraham, even though God had the power to that which he was desiring—a child, but God, first of all, needed him to believe that He God was able to do it. The moment Abraham believed God, it was accounted to his accord as righteousness. This was what created the pathway for him to receive the very promise of God. You see, even the promises of God are limited without our faith. Faith is very essential and we need it to make things happen.

Abraham for example, when he walked in faith, that was the turning point. God became so interested in the guy to a point He called him His friend. What a great reward! This makes us see that faith will always pay. God so enjoyed Abraham that He will come from heaven to discuss with him. Abraham was not in Sodom and Gomorra, but when God wanted to destroy the place, He came and was discussing the fate of the people to Abraham. That tells you the level of trust that was built. In the same way, when we learn the concept of faith, we build that trust and bridge so that God can share deep things with us. The secrets of the Lord are always with those who fear Him and believe in Him.

Jacob who also learned this very concept of faith had a great reward. He stepped out of his father's house seeking a place of refuge, but when he learned the concept of faith, he was greatly rewarded. God so blessed him that he prospered in strange lands. This makes us know that God will equally prosper anyone of us if we can believe Him. Our faith in God is always going to pay off. No matter the circumstances, we have to learn to believe in God. That is the way to getting the divine ushering us into greater experiences.

Understand, friend, that no faith is ever wasted. God is always going to pay off. Like I shared with you that I have come this far and I can tell you that faith is always going to be rewarded. Throughout my life and now that I am entering my eightieth year, I can tell you that faith is always going to pay off. The moment you understand this, your life will move beyond economic recessions, and what is happening in and around you. You will just discover that you are living a life that is full of glory and honor.

At this age that I am in, the Lord has honored me in many ways. This is why I am admonishing you that you have to continue to believe that Lord. remember also, your faith in God doesn't have to be based on circumstances. Many people believe in God because of what they can get from Him, and not who He is. The moment your faith is based on only provision and intervention, then you cannot be rooted and grounded in the fullness of His power. The way to go about Him is to believe Him for who He is.

I am writing to you as a mother and a grandmother to you and I want you to understand that God is never going to fail anyone who places his or her trust in Him. Be encouraged to believe God and He is going to usher you into new seasons of life. The way to secure safety in this life is with the Lord. There is no safety anywhere in this world. We have to seek exemption and the exemption is in the kingdom of God. The only surest safety is found in the kingdom and the way to access the glory in the kingdom is through faith and also consecrated walk with God.

This is the reason why I am encouraging you to keep walking with God. Whatever circumstance you are facing doesn't matter. God is still on the throne and He is going to fulfill all that He has promised you in time. Be encouraged and know that God has got you covered. In the next chapter, I am going to be sharing with you that your circumstances cannot dethrone God. Whatever you are dealing with cannot unmake God. God has been there and He is still going to be there no matter what each one of us is dealing with. The earliest we learn to believe in Him and we can find our comfort in life and safety. Come with me as we dive deeper.

CHAPTER THREE

CIRCUMSTANCES CANNOT DETHRONE GOD

"God is like a mirror, consistent, stable, unchanging; reflecting His image of us, that is always changing."

Anthony Liccione

There are many people who think that what they are going through is ever going to change God or He doesn't even exist. That is the greatest deception from the pits of hell. You see, the devil is always looking for an opportunity to put you in a position where you cannot be helped. This is why He induces this very concept. He does that to make sure that is not in link with God and then He gains an advantage. We have to learn from this very concept and rule as kings and priests in this realm and the kingdom to come.

God is not a modern-day philosophy. He is beyond philosophy. God is beyond science and time. He has always been there before all things came into existence or will ever be in this life. He doesn't change. There are track records of the existence of God and how He has helped man come out of challenges. Therefore, we are going to be wrong if we lose faith in God now because of what we might be dealing with. Just because He didn't come on time doesn't mean He is not in place or He doesn't know what He is doing. God is always on time and He knows what is good for you. just like the case of Lazarus the brother of Mary and Martha. They sent for Jesus when their brother was sick and Jesus didn't show up early. It was funny why Jesus will demonstrate that attitude. It was clearly known that Lazarus was His friend.

However, when Jesus heard that His friend, Lazarus was sick, He stayed two more days. Whatever He was doing there, it was not stated for us to know. But we know that God allowed those circumstances so that He will gain glory after all. Looking at how all the events played out, we can see that God still got the glory.

In the minds of Martha and Mary, and the people around who knew that they walked together and did things together, they would be wondering why Jesus didn't show up in the challenging times they were facing and He claimed they were His friend. What do friends do? They help one another in challenging times. But in this case, Jesus wasn't coming instantly, instead, he stayed two more days. He was delaying the whole process. The question is: why did He have to stay two more days? We will get the answer. Let's look into this text:

"Now a certain [man] was sick, [named] Lazarus, of Bethany, the town of Mary and her sister Martha. (It was [that] Mary which anointed the Lord with ointment, and wiped his feet with her hair, whose brother Lazarus was sick.) Therefore his sisters sent unto him, saying, Lord, behold, he whom thou lovest is sick. When Jesus heard [that], he said, This sickness is not unto death, but for the glory of God, that the Son of God might be glorified thereby. Now Jesus loved Martha, and her sister, and Lazarus. When he had heard therefore that he was sick, he abode two days still in the same place where he was."—(John 11:1—6)

This text clearly reveals that Jesus loved them so much. And the messenger who was sent to give Jesus the information also made it very clear of this same assertion. He said to Him that, "Lord, behold, he whom thou lovest is sick..." Do you see it there? This love was very clear to everyone in and around the city. Everyone knew that and was very aware that Jesus had a deep connection for this very family. Now, this family was going through a challenging time, and Jesus wasn't there. What a shock!

Interestingly, when Jesus heard the story of how His friend was sick, He didn't rush there immediately, but He stayed two more days. Why? That God might receive the glory at the end of all things. Jesus waited for them to exhaust all their human abilities and then He stepped in. the moment everything was gone, then Jesus said they should go and see Him.

Did you notice that His love for Him didn't negate the circumstances? Why would you love someone and allow Him to be going through circumstances that claimed his life? In as much as Jesus loved him, as he was dealing with the challenges, the heart of Jesus was with him in the midst of all the challenging times. While He was away, His heart was with Lazarus. And just because Lazarus was going through challenges doesn't mean that God wasn't available. Jesus was available and He wanted to show the world that God was still in place.

Have you been in a situation where it seemed that you were promised greatness and that God was with you and He loved you so much but the challenges you were dealing with were defying that reality? Have you been in that state where your ordeals were overriding your prophecy? If you have been there, then to you God has sent me to today. It means that you need to be reminded that what you are going through cannot dethrone God. God has always been there and He will always be there. And be reminded that even when you were going through what you were going through, God has been with you in all the situations.

You might ask, "Pastor Lola, where was God when my father was dying? Where was God when I couldn't pay my rent? Where was God when all hell was breaking loosed on me? Where was God when my father was beating us up? Where was God when I almost died of cancer? Where was God when I got fired from the job?" Maybe these are your questions and you are wondering God is out of the throne and all that you read about Him is not true, I need you to know that God was with you in the storm. Maybe this will clear your understanding.

"But now thus saith the Lord that created thee, O Jacob, and he that formed thee, O Israel, Fear not: for I have redeemed thee, I

have called [thee] by thy name; thou [art] mine. When thou passest through the waters, I [will be] with thee; and through the rivers, they shall not overflow thee: when thou walkest through the fire, thou shalt not be burned; neither shall the flame kindle upon thee. For I [am] the Lord thy God, the Holy One of Israel, thy Saviour: I gave Egypt [for] thy ransom, Ethiopia and Seba for thee. Since thou wast precious in my sight, thou hast been honourable, and I have loved thee: therefore will I give men for thee, and people for thy life."— (Isaiah 43:1—4)

Did you see that there? He created you. Now understand here He called you His own and that is comforting and refreshing. That means that you are God's possession and a treasure to Him. And He has redeemed and consecrated you as His own. The moment you see and hear that you are the Lord's that should settle that He is never going to turn His back on you. Challenges might be on your, but it doesn't negate the fact that you are loved by God. You are the Lord's. Therefore, whether you live or die, you live and die to the Lord.

Now here is the mind-blowing truth! He said that when you go through the fire and the water, He is going to be with you. Did He say that when you go through the fire He is going to turn His back on you? Did He said that when you are in the fire or the water He is not going to give you His hand? Did He say that He is going to allow you to perish? Never. The assurance is very clear here that whatever circumstance you are dealing with, He is there with you and ushering you into His purpose. While you are stroking in the darkness, He the Lord is there with you as well and you are never alone in that very place. Grasp this into your spirit and it is ever going to change your perspective about God. This will have peace of mind and heart to be able to sail through life. The moment you are in a challenge, you know that you are not alone there and you sail with all of heaven.

Allow this to settle your doubts. Having this understanding, comfort, and peace of mind returns and you know even in the pain, the Lord is with you and that is never going to overtake you.

Coming back to the Lazarus story, you can see that Jesus loved them, but they were going through challenges. His love was still demonstrated when they were overcome by the challenges. Even in the death, Jesus demonstrated He was in love with them. God's love for you is eternal love. Just as God is eternal, His love is eternal. Therefore, there is nothing you are going through that is going to dethrone Him. Understand this as quickly as you can. It will save you from a lot of emotional stress.

He Is In The Challenge

When Jesus finally decided that He was going to see them after two days, we can see that when appeared there, Martha said something to Him. She said, "… Lord, if thou hadst been here, my brother had not died. But I know, that even now, whatsoever thou wilt ask of God, God will give [it] thee." She knew that Jesus's presence could have overturned the challenges. Her words here meant that Jesus wasn't with them in the challenge. She was lamenting here that if Jesus was there physically, they were not going to get swallowed up by this challenge they were facing.

Then we can see that Jesus didn't leave her wondering in thoughts. Jesus answered her and said something to her, "Your brother will live again." That means Jesus knew what had happened already. You see, there is nothing that happens to us that is outside of God's knowledge. Before anything happens in time, God is always aware of it. This makes us know that God is all-knowing. The reason that name is in place is that He is the only One who knows all things. So, there is nothing happening in this world that is outside of God's knowledge—including what you are dealing with now.

Jesus walked straight to where the gentleman, Lazarus was buried. For four days he was in the grave. Where was God? A simple touch of Jesus could have ended that sickness? But God was not silent about that. Jesus was there with them. His heart was there. The result was what Jesus was looking at. That He might gain the glory. If you look at how Lazarus came back to life, you will discover that Jesus didn't suffer to raise him. He thanked God for raising up for the people. And then He called him out of the grave and He came out. Hallelujah!

As you are reading this book now, you might be dealing with challenges and hard times now and you are wondering where is God in these challenges? You might be asking, "God why are you allowing me to be facing all these that are hard to face?" God is there with you. In the challenges, He is there with you. Understand this and you will be halfway overcoming those challenges. Having a knowing the Lord is on your side, will bring you to a place of eternal rest and faith. Glory!

The answer to that question of yours is that God is with you in the challenges. Just as I used that very portion of scripture in Isaiah 43:1—4, you will know that God is with you in the challenges. You are never alone in the challenges. The presence of the challenges or storms doesn't connote God's absence. Trust me, it is your circumstance and challenge God is going to use to demonstrate His power and strengthen your faith. Never think He is going to leave you in that storm. He is rather going to use that storm to prove His power to you. Each circumstance we face; is what God is going to teach us the concept of faith.

Be encouraged to walk with God. God is never going to fail you in any way. His plans and purposes for your life are so sure and exercising faith in them will help you to rise above the circumstances. Keep reminding yourself that you are never alone. There is never going to come a time where God is going to leave you alone. No! He is always going to be there with you even in the challenges. So, believe and keep walking with God. Never lose trust because of what you are going through. When you don't understand, keep walking with God. When you are in need, keep walking with God. Your faith in God will always bring you a great reward at the end of all things.

He Is Not Changing In The Storm

This is something I have proven over time. And I have come to know and realize that God is never going to change. No matter what we are dealing with in life, none of those can change God in any way. He is God and He will always be God. His power has no end and His ways are past finding. It will also be complete foolishness to think there is no God. The psalmist says that it is only a fool who will think there is no God. God is the One who created all things that we see. And He created all things for His glory and pleasure.

God doesn't run out of power as well. Throughout the lexicons of the universe, there is only one person who has the power to survive ages and centuries. God sustains all but He is sustained by none. Anyone who gains the wisdom and insight to rely on Him, what happens is that there is a union of power and therefore strength and might are granted the one believing.

"Hast thou not known? hast thou not heard, [that] the everlasting God, the Lord, the Creator of the ends of the earth, fainteth not, neither is weary? [there is] no searching of his understanding. He giveth power to the faint; and to [them that have] no might he increaseth strength. Even the youths shall faint and be weary, and the young men shall utterly fall: But they that wait upon the Lord shall renew [their] strength; they shall mount up with wings as eagles; they shall run, and not be weary; [and] they shall walk, and not faint."—(Isaiah 40:28—31)

Do you see something there? You can read that over and over again and you will gain insight into God. Isaiah looking in the lexicons and in search of someone who had the power to survive ages and centuries and He had a glance and now he wrote this for our learning. He found out that it was only the Everlasting God who doesn't faint and never grows weary. So, his assertion is worth considering.

He further said something that reveals the generosity of God. He said that for all those who have no power and faint, God gives power to them, and to those who have no might, He increases strength. This is leadership! He gives this power and He is never afraid that the power and might are going to be corrupted. Secured leadership is when power can be delegated without fear that it will be corrupted. God is a great leader and when it comes to learning leadership, we have to learn from Him.

Anyone who understands this and then begins to fix his or her eyes on the Lord, He is going to renew their strength and also grant them the ability to reign in glory and power. Sometimes when I look at myself, I see the strength of God at work. And how did that happen? It did on the platform of waiting on the Lord. At seventy-eight, the Lord is still sustaining me and I move about doing things on my own without been carried in and out. This is amazing and it is because the Lord has renewed my strength. God grants everyone that same grace. There is no partiality in God. Anyone who dares believe God, He will usher them to that realm of power and glory. Hallelujah!

Friend, understand that God is never changing in the storm. He is there in the storm as the Ancient of Days, that is, one who doesn't change. So, it is not the situation that is going to freak Him out. Never!

"For I [am] the Lord, I change not; therefore ye sons of Jacob are not consumed."—(Malachi 3:6)

"Jesus Christ the same yesterday, and to day, and for ever."—(Hebrews 13:8)

All these reveal one thing—the unchanging nature of God. God is everlasting. He has been there and He is always going to be there. Even when it comes to that point where this world passes away, God is still going to be God. There is therefore no need of losing confidence in Him. We can count on Him. All those who ever dared to do that were never let down. You can as well put your life in the pipeline and He will watch His word to perform.

God is not going to change in your storm or challenge. Reading through these two verses, you can see that He is never going to change in any way. It is not your circumstance that He is going to change. So, remember that God is always God. Instead of wondering in your mind, keep walking with Him. You are the one who gets helped and changed. Faith changes us and shifts us to new realms altogether. Glory!

Your Pain Cannot Dethrone Him

No matter what you are dealing with, that can never dethrone God. He is an all-time God and He is going to continue to reign in glory and power. You might be dealing with your issue of rent now, but that cannot dethrone God. He is still in charge and He can help you out of the situation. You might be dealing with cancer now, but that cannot dethrone God and He can heal you in a matter of seconds. You might be dealing with a broken marriage now, but that cannot dethrone God. He can help you overcome that within seconds. You might be struggling to get through college, God Is able to help you out. There is nothing that you are dealing with that God cannot help you out.

Remember, what you are going through and what is termed pain cannot dethrone God. God is always God and He will continue to be God. Never allow your circumstances to think God is not in place. The moment you get to that point of questioning His power, then there is a problem. God can and will always help you out. This is why you have to learn to always keep walking with Him. No matter what you are dealing with, you must never let go of your faith. Keep the faith no matter the challenge or circumstances. There are great rewards that come with your faith. Therefore, learning to keep walking with God ushers you into that realm of accessing the rewards.

I did share with you the woman with the issue of blood. That woman actually became an example of what faith can produce. She was dealing with pain for twelve years. Within these twelve years, she spent everything that she had and she couldn't keep up anymore. Hearing about Jesus, she decided that she was going to reach out to Jesus. Indeed, her faith was rewarded. This is the same thing that happens to us when we learn the concept of faith. Thus, learning to trust God irrespective of what we are going through. Doing this will bring nothing but great rewards.

Friend, be encouraged to keep walking in the faith. Eventually, your faith is going to pay off. In the next chapter, I will teach you how to go about it when you are dealing with so much pain in your walk with God. The best way to go about the whole thing is to learn to keep focused on God. That is the way to get distracted from the challenges. The devil wants you to keep looking at what you are going through so that you don't see what is about to come—the glory of God. So, instead of focusing on the challenge, see the God behind the challenge. Come with me as we dive into that.

CHAPTER FOUR

KEEP FOCUSED ON GOD INSTEAD

"Don't focus on the adversity; focus on God. No matter what you go through, stay in faith, be your best each day and trust that God will use it to position you for greatness."

Joel Osteen

One irrefutable fact is that; everyone will encounter one challenge or the other. You see, there is nothing in the Word of God that says that the believer will not go through challenges. The truth of the matter is this, every believer will encounter one challenge or the other. Challenges are part of the faith. And God allows that so that we can grow and increase in the faith. This is very applicable to the way of the eagle. We are called to be like the eagles, that is, to soar high above the winds. However, it must be established that before the eagle attains that ability, that is, to master the wind, it must first learn how to face the wind. In the same way, before we can overcome challenges as believers, we have to go through those challenges to learn the way of those challenges. As we do, we can master them.

The challenge is this: Many people concentrate so much on the challenges that we don't see God. Remember that God never called you to focus on what you are going through. God called you to focus on Him. The dream of God for the believer is for the believer to focus on Him. So, it ails God's heart to see that the believer hasn't harnessed his faith enough to look on to the Lord. This is the same reality Paul wanted to suggest to the church. In Hebrews, he lamented that we lay aside all weight that does easily beset us and focus on the Lord. Let's look at his wordings here:

"Wherefore seeing we also are compassed about with so great a cloud of witnesses, let us lay aside every weight, and the sin which doth so easily beset [us], and let us run with patience the race that is set before us, Looking unto Jesus the author and finisher of [our] faith; who for the joy that was set before him endured the cross, despising the shame, and is set down at the right hand of the throne of God. For consider him that endured such contradiction

56

of sinners against himself, lest ye be wearied and faint in your minds."—(Hebrews 12:1—3)

In this writing, the man of God, Paul asserted that we are been surrounded by a great cloud of witnesses and therefore, we have to lay aside every weight that easily besets us. Understand that the Apostle named it because that possibility is available. There is no way you can be in Christ and there won't be attempts each day for you to sway away from the faith. There are always going to be trials and temptations that will seek to bring you to that place where you are not God-covered. This is what Paul wanted us to avoid. And to make that happen, we have to look to Him—Jesus, the author, and finisher of our faith.

Friend, the only way to secure victory and dominion in our walk with the Lord is when we learn this very concept of looking onto Jesus. Keeping our eyes focused on Jesus gives us the power to overcome. Jesus has set that example for us and we have to follow. There was that time where Jesus looked up to the Father. Looking to the Father, He received every help He needed to fulfill His assignment and purpose on the earth. In the same light and truth, if we are going to fulfill what God has entrusted to us, then we need to look to the Lord.

We must learn to shift our attention from cancer to the Lord. We must learn to shift our attention from the pain to the Lord. We must learn to shift our attention from the lack of money to the Lord. We must shift our attention from the marital challenges and focus on the Lord. We must shift our attention from the health issues and focus on the Lord. As we keep our eyes on the Lord, He will grant us grace to rise above those circumstances. Power for dominance originates from the Lord. So, the way to secure it is by looking to Him.

This is why you are encouraged to lay aside anything that will hinder you from experiencing this glorious life in Christ. From my youth until now, I have seen the hand of the Lord in my life in many ways. Right from the beginning of my life until this season where I am entering my eighth decade, I know God has been involved. I resolved earlier in my life that I was going to look on to the Lord no matter what was happening in and around me. This decision therefore helped me to rise above all the challenges that came my way. These same challenges claimed the life of others, but here I am writing this message and book to you. Be assured that God is never going to let you down. In every way, learn to follow Him—keep walking with Him. The rewards are boundless.

See The God Factor In The Challenges

One thing that can help us stay strong in life is when we learn to see the God factor in the challenges. This is something that when we understand will change everything around us. This understanding prepares our minds to become better and then grants us the courage to confront the situations of life. In every challenge that we face in life, there is always a God factor. How God reaches out to us and then shows us His power is through circumstances. Circumstances are platforms to which God reaches out to us.

Whenever we are faced with one, we have to learn to know that God is using that to reach out to us. A clear example is the life of Joseph. God wanted to raise Joseph to become a great prime minister. How He started the whole thing is that He allowed him to begin to see dreams that were so great. The dreams Joseph was getting had nothing to do with what he was doing at that time. They were revealing the future. In other words, they were insights into the future.

Joseph went on and told his brothers about these dreams. They began to hate him and envy him. Another time, he saw another dream and he went and told his father. His father was so mad and rebuked him. The fact that they were all going to bow before him was surprising to the father. However, that was God's initiative to make that happen.

"And Joseph dreamed a dream, and he told [it] his brethren: and they hated him yet the more. And he said unto them, Hear, I pray you, this dream which I have dreamed: For, behold, we [were] binding sheaves in the field, and, lo, my sheaf arose, and also stood upright; and, behold, your sheaves stood round about, and made obeisance to my sheaf. And his brethren said to him, Shalt thou indeed reign over us? or shalt thou indeed have dominion over us? And they hated him yet the more for his dreams, and for his words. And he dreamed yet another dream, and told it his brethren, and said, Behold, I have dreamed a dream more; and, behold, the sun and the moon and the eleven stars made obeisance to me. And he told [it] to his father, and to his brethren: and his father rebuked him, and said unto him, What [is] this dream that thou hast dreamed? Shall I and thy mother and thy brethren indeed come to bow down ourselves to thee to the earth? And his brethren envied him; but his father observed the saying."— *(Genesis 37:5—11)*

You can go over that text again and you will see the promise of greatness. The promise was there, but the process is not revealed here. You see, destiny involves process and promise. Anytime the promise comes, then there is a process attached to it. We need to know this well. The process God reveals that in time. He never reveals that at a go. This must sink in your spirit.

When Joseph had this dream (the promise) he was so excited about it that he was going about telling everyone about it. Little did he ever know that in that dream was a promise that was going to even threaten his life. He never saw that coming. So, with the dream, he got a first reaction—from his brothers and his father. Each of them gave a negative response to the situation. However, the text revealed that his father observed the saying. What we need to know about fatherhood is that fathers oversee dreams and observe the manifestation of dreams. This is what Jacob was doing here.

Now for the dreams of Joseph to come to pass, God had to create situations to make manifest the promise and that is the process. The situation God placed him in was to reveal the God factor. Remember that the next time you are confronted with or by anything, then you must see the God factor in that very element. Joseph didn't see the prison in the dream. Joseph didn't see betrayal in the dream. Joseph didn't see envy in the dream. Joseph didn't see failures in the dream. Joseph didn't see the disappointment in the dream. What he saw was greatness. God, therefore, had to create circumstances to which the glory of this dream could be harnessed. This explains why Joseph faced what he was facing.

Just for the fulfillment of that dream, he was sold out. Just for the fulfillment of that dream, he was lied upon and was thrown into prison for the wrong thing. He lingered in suffering for years. However, God was working something there behind the scenes. The God-factor there was that God was preparing him for the dream. In other words, God was working on his character and capacity. Anytime we find ourselves in situations, this is what the situations come to do—to prepare our character and capacity for the promise. Hallelujah!

The next time you find yourself in challenging times, you have to see the God factor in that situation. Never allow that circumstance to blind you that you cannot see what God is doing. While Joseph was going through all these ordeals, he knew that there was a God-factor there. He believed in God. It is reported that because of him, the Lord blessed his master. That means he kept the relationship with God. He knew God-factor in the midst of the challenges. You can see his confessions to his brothers. His assertion to his brothers indicates that he knew by revelation what he was dealing with was for good. Glory!

"And his brethren also went and fell down before his face; and they said, Behold, we [be] thy servants. And Joseph said unto them, Fear not: for [am] I in the place of God? But as for you, ye thought evil against me; [but] God meant it unto good, to bring to pass, as [it is] this day, to save much people alive. Now therefore fear ye not: I will nourish you, and your little ones. And he comforted them, and spake kindly unto them."— (Genesis 50:18—21)

Whew! This is the response of one who has mastered over circumstances. Do you know sometimes you can go through a situation and become a slave to that circumstance? That is what many people go through. When they face a betrayal, they are always overcome by that situation. This was not the case for Joseph. Joseph understood that for process and productivity to come continually, he needed to let go of the pain they caused him. You can see his words to his brothers. That means he had grown above the things they did to him. He was not a slave to the deeds of his brothers.

When the actions of people control you, then you are a slave to them. But when it happens otherwise, then you have mastered the situation and the people as well. Joseph did that and that is why he became victorious. He told his brothers that even though when they were doing what they were doing, they were thinking they were hurting him, but God was using those very situations to usher him into the promise. Then he embraced them and showed them.

Joseph had this victory and dominion over the circumstance because he knew that God was involved. This is what happens when we see the God factor in our challenges. That understanding will change the way we handle the pain. And above all, it will help us to respond positively to the things that happened to us. Experience entirely what happens to a man, but what he does with what happens to him.

In our walk with God as well, we have to have this understanding. With this understanding, we can change things in and around us. Knowing that as you are with God, whatever happens, is God coordinated for your favor. This is what Paul knew and no wonder he was able to do so much in the kingdom of God. Paul's life was just such a glorious life. Why? Because of the understanding he had. He knew a lot about God then he saw life from a different perspective. In other words, he saw the God factor in his daily dealings and challenges. Look at his wording here:

"And we know that all things work together for good to them that love God, to them who are the called according to [his] purpose."— (Romans 8:28)

In this very portion, he didn't say that some things work together for those who love God. He used the word, "All things." This connotes that whatever situation or circumstance the believer is passing through, it is for good. Once you come to know the Lord, whatever the situation, it is for the better and greater good. Understand this and then nothing will make you shift your face.

Instead of crying that things are wrong in your life, know that those things that are you are facing in life are for your good and God will turn things around no matter how long it takes. Keep focused and keep walking with the Lord. No matter what you face in life, see the God factor. This insight will usher you into realms that no man can bring you down. Hallelujah!

Picture God And Not The Mountain

Many people amid the challenges, they focus on the mountain that they don't see the God of the mountain. This is something wrong to do. The moment you begin to look or focus on the challenge, what you are doing is that you are giving power to the challenge. That hour where you focus on the challenge, the challenge masters you and therefore it becomes almost impossible to overcome it. What to do to remedy this is learning to focus on God—who is the God of the mountain. He made all things for His pleasure and glory.

When you find yourself dealing with a situation that is beyond control, then you must set yourself in the place of serenity and then focus on God instead of the problem. Faith is very essential in dealing with challenges. Everyone who wants to rise above the challenges must believe in God's ability above the challenges. With God, all things are possible. Understanding this will refresh you and lift your faith so high.

Author and songwriter Max Lucado assert that "Focus on giants - you stumble. Focus on God - Giants tumble." That means that when we focus on the giants, we are never going to get them out of the way. But the moment we focus on God, then things shift as well. The way to deal with challenges in your walk with God is by learning to focus on God. That is that element is seeking to take away from you. keep that intact and never allow anything to sway you away from it. When you do, giants will tremble before you. No circumstance can pin you down. Do you know why? There is an understanding that focus will drift into you. You will come to embrace that the quality of your life is never defined by the circumstances of your life. Your life is worth more than what you are dealing with. Hence, you stay motivated irrespective of the storms.

No storm should cause you to be looking at the storm. What you have to always do is that you have to always pick God and not the storm. Look at God and not the mountain. Look at God and not the challenges. Look at God and not the pain. Look at God and not the lack of money. Look at God and not the rent. Look at God and not the relationship problems. Look at God and not the health issues. When you focus on God and not the mountain, God makes you His focus. When He does, He will shake even the foundations of the world to ensure your well-being.

Stay In Faith Irrespective Of The Challenge

Jesus asserted that faith can move a mountain. He brought us to understand that with little to nothing faith, we can command a mountain to move. And remember I made you understand that the mountain he was talking about is not the physical mountain like Everest, but He was talking about the circumstances of life. What can change your life is faith. Faith is that very thing you need in life. Friend, when you lay hold of faith, it can change everything in and around you. This is why you are often challenged in getting to do things that will build your faith. Because Satan knows that when you grow your faith and gain ground, you will become better and step into greatness. So, wise up now and learn from this so you stay in faith and grow in faith and in the knowledge of Jesus.

"Jesus said unto him, If thou canst believe, all things [are] possible to him that believeth."—(Mark 9:23)

Jesus made this assertion on the condition of the same boy we discussed earlier. This boy was suffering from a lunatic spirit. This spirit will often throw him into the fire or even water. This boy's father came to Jesus seeking help. He didn't see Jesus—He was on the mountain. A few of the disciples were at the bottom of the mountain. They were asked to pray for this gentleman and they couldn't. It went on and on until they gave up. Then Jesus came down and they brought the boy to Jesus. Jesus helped and corrected their error. You might be asking, "Pastor Lola, what was it?" Their faith. They couldn't stay in faith. Jesus, therefore, made this assertion to get them to the place of faith.

The revelation in this assertion is that if we can believe, things can change. As long as we can stay in faith, we can come to that dimension where we can see great manifestations in life. This is what Jesus was teaching us here. So, when you find yourself plagued with challenges and hardness, then something is needed—faith. Faith is what you need to change your circumstances. Gaining faith and increasing in the proportion of the knowledge of God, will propel you to new dimensions and seasons in life altogether.

Stay in faith every single time and keep doing the good things each day and know that God is going to use the very challenges and circumstances you are dealing with and bring you to the place of divine assistance. Most times God gives us challenges so we can come to the place of faith. And coming to faith, circumstances change as well. Hallelujah!

God's vision is to lead you to greatness. Live each day in faith knowing that He is going to usher you into that greatness in a majestic way. Stay in faith with this belief and know that God is not a man. God is not a man that He will promise you and He will not do it. Whatever promise God gives, He is going to honor that promise. So, believe Him and know that what He said concerning you is going to come to pass. No circumstance should shift your faith. Keep walking with God. As you do, you will experience the fullness of the power of God! Glory!

CHAPTER FIVE

HEAVENLY AIDED—DON'T FRET

"You are God's investment and He will protect that at all costs. Circumstances are meant for you to reflect and display the increase of God's investment in you."

Edward Djamome

Nothing is rewarding than knowing that all of heaven is backing you up no matter the circumstance. This assurance and insight are rewarding more than a blank check. You see, many times we linger in challenges because we don't know what is made available to us. Information is a tool for freedom. However, many people don't know this. Hence, they linger in struggle and challenges. That is not supposed to be. The more informed you are, the more you are going to become productive and free. Freedom is in information.

Information is very important that Jesus Himself asserted that we shall know the truth and the truth will set us free. What is truth? Truth is information. Coming to have an access to a certain secret that propels excellence is information. The way to freedom and induce excellence in our lives is the acquisition of information. Knowing is very key and powerful. This is why you will understand that the provision of God is going to be manifested in the proportion of your knowledge.

So, how much of God do you know? How much do you know that God exists to assist you in this life? How much assurance do you have that you are created to dominate in this life? The results you encounter around you are a reflection of the knowledge that you have. You can never experience above the knowledge that you have.

"According as his divine power hath given unto us all things that [pertain] unto life and godliness, through the knowledge of him that hath called us to glory and virtue: Whereby are given unto us exceeding great and precious promises: that by these ye might be partakers of the divine nature, having escaped the corruption that is in the world through lust."—(2 Peter 1:3—4)

This scripture is one of the most quoted texts in the church today. However, there is a portion many done see—that is the ending part. The ending part talks about the proportion of the knowledge of Him. This is the key here. God has made available all things that pertain to life and godliness, but the manifestation of that is through the knowledge of Him that you know. That is to say, these provisions are going to be manifested only in the proportion of your knowledge. So, what we should be doing as believers is learning to grow in the knowledge of Him. This will help us to access the fullness of the provisions of the Cross.

Knowing heaven is assisting you through this life is so rewarding and reviving. No circumstance can shake you or make you lose faith. You walk in confidence and with a renewed mindset.

God Is Out To Fight For You

As I just shared with you that information is very key, knowing that God is for you makes a difference in life. Imperatively, we must understand that knowing that God is out to fight for us, no circumstance can make us give up in life. We can learn the lesson from the people of Israel. Looking at that experience, we can drift so much sense and we can gain understanding in our pursuit of increase and impact.

"And when Pharaoh drew nigh, the children of Israel lifted up their eyes, and, behold, the Egyptians marched after them; and they were sore afraid: and the children of Israel cried out unto the Lord. And they said unto Moses, Because [there were] no graves in Egypt, hast thou taken us away to die in the wilderness? wherefore hast thou dealt thus with us, to carry us forth out of Egypt? [Is] not this the word that we did tell thee in Egypt, saying, Let us alone, that we may serve the Egyptians? For [it had been]

better for us to serve the Egyptians, than that we should die in the wilderness. And Moses said unto the people, Fear ye not, stand still, and see the salvation of the Lord, which he will shew to you to day: for the Egyptians whom ye have seen to day, ye shall see them again no more for ever. The Lord shall fight for you, and ye shall hold your peace. "—(Exodus 14:10—14)

This text is a revelation of how much God is willing to fight for us when we are in troubled circumstances. The people of Israel were walking in the promise of God—that is, entering the Promised land that God vowed to their fathers. Now, the moment they came out of Egypt the land of bondage, something began to happen, the people of Egypt began to follow them up again. This is the reason when they were leaving, they plundered that nation to nothing. Egypt was one of the richest nations in the world. They went bankrupt after the Lord fought the nation because they touched the firstborn of God. From then until now, they have not recovered from that recession. This is the warning to anyone who wants to stand in the way of the Lord. When the Lord sets to fight you, you cannot recover from that damage.

We see this clear example where. When Israel left Egypt, the Egyptians followed them and they didn't want them to come out. The people of Israel lifted their eyes and saw them coming from behind and at that time, they had come up to the Red sea. They went to Moses and began to complain and murmur. They said that is it because there were no graves in Egypt that is why Moses brought them out for them to die. They were crying and had lost hope. Moses now began to speak up to them. As a leader, he had to stop the tension that was creeping into them. He told them that they should stand still and see the salvation of God. After stilling the people, he went to see the Lord about it. God showed him what to do.

You see, God is ever willing to help us overcome whatever challenge we are dealing with, however, we must be willing to call on Him for help. The Bible accords that anyone who calls on the name of the Lord shall be saved (See Romans 10:13). This indicates that God is never going to turn a wearied soul away. He showed that nature here. When Moses prayed to the Lord in distress, God answered him. What happened? You might be asking. God parted the Red Sea and they walked on dry ground. He wanted for the last person of Israel to leave the water and the last person of Egypt to enter the water, then He closed it up.

This was the day God destroyed the Egyptian army. It was outermost destruction that came on them. This brings us the understanding that God is out to fight for us. All of heaven is willing to support us overcome the challenges of life. We must know this so that when we are faced with the challenges of life, we can know where and whom to run to. We who have believed in the name of the Lord, don't despair because we know that God is always going to fight for us. This occurrence that happened is a lighter to us that God is out to fight for us.

We can see another instance we can learn from that God is out to fight for us is looking at the life of Hezekiah. He was a great man who knew the Lord and counsels of the Lord. As he was reigning as a king, it came to pass that King of Assyria, Sennacherib made a mockery of the people of Israel and boasted of how he was going to conquer that territory. When Hezekiah heard this, he rent his clothes and began to weep before the Lord. He made a declaration that we can learn from, he said that the time for the woman to deliver was upon them, but there was no strength to bring forth the baby. This was talking about the situation they were in as a people.

Israel as a nation is great. The promise over Israel is great. The manifestation of those promises comes with a price. That is the comparison the man is speaking about here. His assertion means that it was time for Israel to deliver her promise, but there was no strength and they had to call on the Lord for help. Let's look at the words:

"And it came to pass, when king Hezekiah heard [it], that he rent his clothes, and covered himself with sackcloth, and went into the house of the Lord. And he sent Eliakim, which [was] over the household, and Shebna the scribe, and the elders of the priests, covered with sackcloth, to Isaiah the prophet the son of Amoz. And they said unto him, Thus saith Hezekiah, This day [is] a day of trouble, and of rebuke, and blasphemy: for the children are come to the birth, and [there is] not strength to bring forth. It may be the Lord thy God will hear all the words of Rab–shakeh, whom the king of Assyria his master hath sent to reproach the living God; and will reprove the words which the Lord thy God hath heard: wherefore lift up [thy] prayer for the remnant that are left."—(2 Kings 19:1—4)

Hezekiah was very wise enough. Under his government and administration, they had come to crossroads and the way he chose to remedy the situation was to make an alliance with the Lord. This is why he involved the prophet. He knew the job of the prophet is to pray for the people. Understand that intercession is an integral part of the prophetic ministry. This is why it is very dangerous for someone to call himself or herself a prophet when he or she doesn't know the way to pray. We are all prone to deception when we don't know the way of intercession. This king understood that and in this distress, he engaged the prophet Isaiah.

Isaiah, therefore, gave them comforting words that God was going to fight for them. And that stilled the people. However, Hezekiah didn't just also rest on the words of the prophet. He went further into the place of prayer again. This talks to us about how each one of us must learn to build a personal prayer life. Let's look at that now:

"And Hezekiah received the letter of the hand of the messengers, and read it: and Hezekiah went up into the house of the Lord, and spread it before the Lord. And Hezekiah prayed before the Lord, and said, O Lord God of Israel, which dwellest [between] the cherubims, thou art the God, [even] thou alone, of all the kingdoms of the earth; thou hast made heaven and earth. Lord, bow down thine ear, and hear: open, Lord, thine eyes, and see: and hear the words of Sennacherib, which hath sent him to reproach the living God. Of a truth, Lord, the kings of Assyria have destroyed the nations and their lands, And have cast their gods into the fire: for they [were] no gods, but the work of men's hands, wood and stone: therefore they have destroyed them. Now therefore, O Lord our God, I beseech thee, save thou us out of his hand, that all the kingdoms of the earth may know that thou [art] the Lord God, [even] thou only."—(2 Kings 19:14—19)

Hezekiah took the letter that was written to the house of the Lord. He laid the letter before the Lord asking that the Lord will read the letter and help them. He beckoned and called on the Lord to prove Himself so that nations will know that He alone was God among all the kingdoms of the earth. And indeed, when God looked at how Hezekiah honored Him and also how he respected the prophet, He answered that prayer. Let's see how God responded to this prayer.

"And it came to pass that night, that the angel of the Lord went out, and smote in the camp of the Assyrians an hundred fourscore and five thousand: and when they arose early in the morning,

behold, they [were] all dead corpses. So Sennacherib king of Assyria departed, and went and returned, and dwelt at Nineveh. And it came to pass, as he was worshipping in the house of Nisroch his god, that Adrammelech and Sharezer his sons smote him with the sword: and they escaped into the land of Armenia. And Esar-haddon his son reigned in his stead. "— *(2 Kings 19:35—37)*

This is so amazing! God sent an angel from His presence and the angel to come and fight for the king. When the Assyrians woke up in the morning, they saw only dead people. They didn't see how they were slain. The Lord did that. God came out and fought for them. God is still doing the same today. He still fights for His people. This is why I want to encourage you to keep walking with God. God is out to fight for you no matter the circumstances. You are heavenly aided and therefore you don't have to fret in the circumstances. No circumstance can kill you without your permission.

God Is With You Don't Fret

We must know that God is with us no matter the circumstance. The assurance that the Lord gave us is not that He is going to be with us, but He is with us. That means it is already with happened glory to God. The insight is this: Even before you step into the situation, the Lord is there with you in that situation and He grants you grace to overcome. That means under His watch, no circumstance or situation can overtake you. Glory!

"But now thus saith the Lord that created thee, O Jacob, and he that formed thee, O Israel, Fear not: for I have redeemed thee, I have called [thee] by thy name; thou [art] mine. When thou passest through the waters, I [will be] with thee; and through the rivers, they shall not overflow thee: when thou walkest through the fire, thou shalt not be burned; neither shall the flame kindle upon thee.

For I [am] the Lord thy God, the Holy One of Israel, thy Saviour: I gave Egypt [for] thy ransom, Ethiopia and Seba for thee. Since thou wast precious in my sight, thou hast been honourable, and I have loved thee: therefore will I give men for thee, and people for thy life." — (Isaiah 43:1—4)

These words came from the Lord and not a mortal man. If it had been a man, then we could somehow doubt the assertions, but this is from the Lord. Therefore, we have to take those words with all seriousness knowing that God cannot lie and He is not a son of man wherein He can repent. In these words that He communicated to Isaiah the prophet, He made it very clear that we are His treasured possession and He knows us by our names. That means that nothing can happen to us without His awareness. This we must establish within us.

Then He went on to talk about the circumstances where we go through. He said that even though we go through the fire, the fire will not burn, and neither shall the flames kindle upon us. And even though we go through the water, they shall not overflow us. What does that communicate? Divine preservation. God has promised to preserve us His own treasured possession.

Now with this great assurance, why would you go through life as if there is no one for you? We must build our confidence in the Lord and the fullness of His promises. Many of us can believe the word of our doctor but we cannot believe the assurance of the Lord. This is what the Lord said He is going to do. What we have to do is believe Him for that word and we will emerge victoriously.

In that text you read, you will notice that God asserted His love for you. It is on the account of that love that He brings you to that place of divine preservation. When you love someone, you will not allow them to go through challenges. You will do everything possible to make sure that they are saved and preserved. That is what the Lord is doing on the account of His love for us. This even can be seen in the way He sacrificed to save us from sin. He so loved the world that He gave Jesus and that whosoever believes in Him will not perish, but have eternal life. Glory!

This same Jesus when He came, He communicated the fullness of the love of God for us. Now, He went into hell and conquered death. That day when He rose, all of heaven held its breath until that stone was rolled away. He conquered death and triumphed over sin. After this victory, He gave a great assurance before He went to heaven. He said that He is going to be with us even to the end of the age (See Mathew 28:18—20).

Did He said He is going to be with us for one week? Did He said that He is going to be with us for one month and then stop looking after us? Never. His words are, "to the end of the age." That is talking about the end of the world. We need to know that God is always going to be taking care of us no matter what. Whatever circumstance you might be in now, understand that you are never there alone. God is there with you in it. You might be struggling to pay your house rent now, you are not doing that alone. He is there with you. You might be dealing with a terminal disease now and you are wondering where the Lord is, don't fret. He is there with you. Things might be working against you for a season, you have to know that God is there with you.

There is nothing that we can go through that can negate the presence of God in our lives. Even in the greatest darkness, we have to know that God is there. This is the same confidence that David had in Psalms 23 when he asserted that even though he walks through the valley of the shadow of death, he is not going to fear any evil. Why? Because the Lord is with Him. When the Lord is with you, what happens is that you walk in confidence. You just don't fret at all.

This is what I want you to know as you are reading through this book that you are heavenly aided and there should never be room to be afraid. Fear is not good for you. Fear is the undoing of men. Knowing this, we can rest on the promises of God. God cannot lie and we have to believe that so that we can walk in courage and confidence. God lends us His hand and strength in the midst of the challenges. So, we have must never give room for any doubts or fear in life. Hallelujah!

Heaven Supported All Times

When you read about the story of Moses and the children of Israel and how they crossed the Red sea, you noticed that God came in even when they thought they were never going to make it through. God came in the fullness of His glory and turned that muddy ground into dry land and they walked on it. What is that? Power and faithfulness. It tells us that God is committed to all of us our well-being. He has not called us out of darkness to leave or desert us in the storm. He is always going to come through for us to assist us to get over the very circumstances of life.

And then we saw another incidence in the days of Hezekiah and how the Lord sent an angel to come from heaven to fight for the nation Israel. You see, when you believe in the Lord, be assured of something that you are always heavenly supported at all times. Whatever you go through in life can never undo His love or promises and He will go any length to make sure you are safe.

In the days of Jesus, He was in the boat with His disciples when they were overtaken by a squall. They went to Jesus and started lamenting and crying, "Don't you care we are perishing?" When Jesus got up, He didn't talk about what they were saying, He rather demonstrated His love for them. That is, He showed them that He was for them and not against them. Hence, He rebuked the storm.

"And the same day, when the even was come, he saith unto them, Let us pass over unto the other side. And when they had sent away the multitude, they took him even as he was in the ship. And there were also with him other little ships. And there arose a great storm of wind, and the waves beat into the ship, so that it was now full. And he was in the hinder part of the ship, asleep on a pillow: and they awake him, and say unto him, Master, carest thou not that we perish? And he arose, and rebuked the wind, and said unto the sea, Peace, be still. And the wind ceased, and there was a great calm. And he said unto them, Why are ye so fearful? how is it that ye have no faith? And they feared exceedingly, and said one to another, What manner of man is this, that even the wind and the sea obey him?" — (Mark 4:35—41)

Did you notice the event here? Jesus had just finished performing a miracle of feeding them, and now He asked that they go to the other side. And there was a challenge. What that means is that in life, when you are going nowhere, you don't encounter challenges. Challenges come your way when you are trying to make progress. Progress induces and invites adversity. This is what happened here. They were trying to get to the other side and there was a squall that came contrary to them.

While they were on that journey, something happened incredibly. Jesus slept off. Maybe because of the stress of ministering to the people and all that. While He was resting, storms came and they went to Jesus crying and beckoning on Him saying, "Master, don't you care that we are perishing?" Jesus got up and rebuked the wind. And instantly the winds stopped billowing. They were in shock and they kept asking one another, "What manner of man is this, that even the wind and the sea obey him?"

Understand that you are never alone in your circumstance as you are walking with the Lord. You have to keep walking with the Lord no matter what. Keep walking knowing that you are heavenly supported at all times and there is no room for fear and doubts. All of heaven is supporting you to overcome the hard circumstances. Know this and you will be stirred in the faith always to press in the midst of the challenges. Remember that God brings the challenges so that you can see Him. In as much as those challenges are not pleasurable, but God reveals certain dimensions of Himself in those circumstances.

He is a God of intervention and He can intervene in circumstances. Be assured of that. Know that God is a God who supports. Once He is in heaven, everything in heaven supports you. If the Lord be on your side, everything in and around you can become a weapon the Lord will use to intervene in your situation. Know this and keep walking. Fight forward and don't look back. Many people look back when they are confronted with circumstances and challenges. You have to look forward without any doubts or restrains within you. Hallelujah!

Heaven is working for you and not against you. If this truth could just sink into your spirit, you will be stunned by the impact and influence you are going to make in this realm. You are not going to be waiting in fear, but you will take incredible leaps because you know who is on your side. In the days of Elisha, an army was sent to take him captive, but before they got there, God had sent angels to fill the mountains up. Chariots surrounded the man of God. His servant didn't see that, but the man of God was at peace because he knew who was on His side. He even prayed that the servant might have the same experience. Friend, know that God would not allow you to be overtaken by the circumstances of life. Keep walking with Him. All of heaven is out to defend you and make sure you fulfill your purpose in the earth realm. Be strong and then keep walking with God. Great rewards are awaiting you in Christ Jesus. Hallelujah!

CHAPTER SIX

ASSURED PROMISES

"The system of Christianity is hanging on the balance of realities and promises. The joy is that we can count on them."

Edward Djamome

E verything that makes Christianity we can count on them. Because the one who pioneered it can be counted on and that is God. We can trust the Lord because He cannot lie. We have seen and known that God is not like a man and therefore we can count on Him and His Word. We must understand that we are believing one that we can rely on. Everyone in this world has the tendency of failing in one way or the other, but God cannot and will never fail anyone. As long as you keep believing and following Him, He is never going to fail you.

Most times the reason we are not experiencing the realities of the Word of God and that of the Lord is that we are not walking in His way. We are either deserting His ordinances or we are walking outside it. The misalignment will make us not experience the glory of the promises of God. The way to remedy this is by learning to find our way back to Him. Above all, we have to believe Him again.

"God [is] not a man, that he should lie; neither the son of man, that he should repent: hath he said, and shall he not do [it]? or hath he spoken, and shall he not make it good?" — (Numbers 23:19)

God had promised the people of Israel that He was going to take them to a land that was flowing with milk and honey. This is a land that is often called the Promised land. This was a promise that was given to the people. For many years before this particular generation came into existence. But God in the fullness of time came to redeem this very promise. And as the people came out of the nation Egypt and they were going into that Promised land. This king went and hired Balaam to curse the people. Little did he know that the Lord was on their side. God was fighting for them to fulfill His promise to them.

While this guy was asked to curse them, the Lord was constraining him from cursing and he rather blessed them instead. When he lifted up his eyes and looked at Israel in their camps, he saw the Lord in their midst. He asserted that there was a shout of a king in their midst. That tells us that the Lord was there. What was He doing there? He was ensuring the manifestation of the promise. He was protecting the promise so that no one could sabotage the promise.

Then Balaam after trying many times and couldn't go further; made this very assertion that the Lord is not like a human being who is going to change or lie. Therefore, what He had told Israel, there was going to be a manifestation of it and the people were going to inherit their promise.

What can we learn from this very story? We can see that whatever God has promised, we can count on that promise. Throughout the scriptures, there is no single promise that God gave that didn't come to pass. Everything that He said was going to happen, did happen. Therefore, we have to become convinced that if the Lord said He is going to be with us and bless us, then we have to keep walking with Him and not looking at the circumstances around us. Sometimes there can be these great promises, but the circumstances can be so challenging that you can begin to think that God is not with you. But we can count on the promises of God. Because they are sure!

He Has Promised To Take Care Of You

God's promise to you is to take good care of you and all that is yours. He has promised to take care of everything that concerns you. When He said that He was going to be with you, He meant that He was going to be taking care of everything that concerns your life.

So, friend, be encouraged to know that what the Lord has promised you, there is going to be a manifestation of that promise.

God has promised to take care of your health. He doesn't want you to walk in sickness and all of that. That is why He sent Jesus for you. Jesus received the beatings for you. By the stripes of Jesus, you were healed. This is a reality and a promise as well. As you are awakened to the beauty of that reality, then you experience it. For the time being, as you are still on the earth, He has promised to protect you and make sure that you are in sound health. Hallelujah!

Many people don't even know God wants them well. God wants you well and healthy. I have stood on these promises for many years. I am almost eighty years at the time of this writing and therefore, I know that whatever God has said is ever going to come to pass and we can count on it. The reason is that God has a clear track record of keeping His promises. I have stood on these promises all my life. And God has been so good to me. I have walked in the glory of it. At eighty, I am still doing things on my own and have not been carried in and out. I still go and minister and out as everyone other person does.

This is nothing but the goodness of God. There are many people who have never even reached my age and then laid its icy hand on them. But the Lord has blessed me tremendously. He has made me a great grandmother. Hallelujah!

I am writing this not to fill you up with plenty and wonderful revelation, but I write to encourage you that you can count on the promises of God. The promises of God are assured. So, believe and keep walking with God. It doesn't matter what you might be encountering now, all that the Lord has told you are going to come to pass without fail. What you have to do is keep walking with the

Lord. As you do, you are repositioning yourself to experience the glory of all the promises.

He has promised to take care of your health. He has promised to take care of your finances. He has promised to take care of your business. He has promised to take care of your ministry. He has promised to take care of your marriage. He has promised to defend your children. He has promised to protect your investments. He has promised to bless the works of your hands. He has promised to be there for you even in the darkest hour. Everything that concerns you, God has promised to take care of it. That is how much He loves you. He loves you to a point that He is willing to make sure you are well catered for. So, believe Him.

His Track Record Speaks

God has got a great track record of performing all that He has promised His people. When we read through from Genesis to Revelation, it is the compendium of the track record of God's fulfilling of the promises He made at some point to one person or the other. These works and promises are written so that we can refer to His track record to find consolations in Him. Paul in his writing to the church in Philippi spoke about these consolations in Christ. That means that we have to look at the promises of God to find great solace and consolation (See Philippians 2:1)

It is not now that God is going to establish Himself about His promises. There is already a track record of His doings and works. Hence, we will be unwise to ignore those doings. Personally, I have come to encounter these promises and it has revolutionized my life. From my health even to the ministry, God promised and each of the promises has come to pass. Everything the Lord assured me from my young age until now, all has come to fruition. This communicates nothing but His faithfulness and ability to fulfill all that He has promised.

So, whatever the Lord has said to you, I need you to know that God cannot lie. I already established that reality to you that He is not a man that He should lie. Hence, you need to know that whatever promises He has given you, you have to know that they are assured and you should believe them as you walk with Him. Never come to that place where you doubt His promises. Whatever God has told you in secret or through a prophet, you have to know that they are going to come to pass. Anytime you are losing faith, go back to the scripture. It has a lot of the promises of God that came to pass.

Just for example, when you look at the coming of Jesus. From the time of Adam when God promised the coming of Jesus. Everyone that came after spoke about this coming. God never lied about that issue. Many men who witnessed that reality in their spirit communicated it in the volumes of their writings. It came to pass as the Lord had predetermined it. Jesus came and died and also resurrected as it was prophesied. Indeed, He became a ransom for the sin of mankind. Through His coming, we are made at peace with God and we have access to the presence of God and we have become heirs of the kingdom and also partakers of the inheritance of the saints and His divine nature. Isn't this glorious?

Jesus' coming fulfilled all that God spoke about. Remember that it had to do with the life of His Son. Irrespective of how precious the life of Jesus was, as far as God promised, He had to release Him to die and bring man redemption. So, friend, if there is a promise of God over your life, there is something you need to know, and that is, you can count on that promise. Because God has a track record of fulfilling all that He has promised. Dare to believe all that the Lord has said. Anyone who was in that position, that is, believing in the Lord was never disappointed. Put your life in that life, that is, believing in the Lord. The rewards are boundless. Glory!

Be Assured And Walk Forward

Be assured of the promises made to you. When the Lord spoke to me about the New Glory International Ministries, there is something I knew and that is, as the Lord spoke, it was going to come to pass no matter what. Indeed, in the fullness of time, God fulfilled all that He has promised. We have not yet stepped into the fullness of the promise He gave concerning the ministry. Even if I don't live to see it, He is still going to honor that promise. It is by His counsel that ministry came to being. That means He is going to fulfill His part of the bargain as we are also doing our part.

Why am I sharing this with you, I am so that you can gain that understanding that God is never going to lie. When God says something to you, you have to be assured and moves forward. It is most times challenging to secure a message from the Lord, but when you do, it changes everything.

In John chapter 9, there is a story of a man that was born blind. He was left on the streets to beg. It came to pass that as he was there, he had an encounter with Jesus. As he did, Jesus asked him to go and wash at the Pool of Siloam. He went and washed and was well. People began to wonder how he got healed. They went and asked him how he got healed. The Pharisees posed the question, "Hey, man, can you tell us what happened to you? We need to know what happened." He didn't know who healed him. So, he answered a certain man healed him. Now later Jesus found him in the temple and asked him about Himself. The man now gained an understanding of the Person of Jesus.

After gaining that understanding and revelation of Jesus, He went back to them and told them it was Jesus. This got them so mad and they were begun to fight amongst themselves. They called Jesus a sinner. Some of them said that a sinner couldn't do any miracle. That man further said, "Whether he is a sinner or not, one thing I do know is this, I was once blind, and now I can see." Hallelujah!

You can read the story in John 9. It is such an amazing text. Now, you might be asking why I brought that up. I did so that you can see the way the man responded to the word of Jesus. He just met Jesus and by then he didn't have an understanding of Him. He asked him to go to the pool and wash and then that was it. He believed and moved towards it. That is the way we are supposed to respond to the promises of God. We have to be assured and then move forward. Once the Lord said it, then we have to take that word and run with it. We don't have to remain stationary because things are not going our way. We have to work on the Word. It is in engaging in the Word of God that we can harness the glory in the Word.

All the promises of God over your life, be assured of them, and walk forward. And when I am talking about walking forward, I am as well talking about the hard situations. Walking forward means that they are going to be challenges and hard times, but you match towards the goal. That is what we are supposed to do if we are going to experience the glory of our sonship. That is, we must keep looking at the goal. The goal is becoming like Jesus—conforming to the very image of Christ. This should be the goal of every believer.

So, be assured of everything that God has said. As you are marching forward, Satan might throw in some things, but you have to look beyond them all. He will throw in sicknesses, financial situations, and conflicts with people, and even trials and temptations, but you need to look beyond them all and keep moving. No circumstance should sake you away from the faith or get you distracted. Mostly, that is always the goal of the challenges, to distract you from purpose. But you have to keep moving and pressing forward knowing that everything God said to you is coming to pass with no delay! Hallelujah!

CHAPTER SEVEN

KEEP THE PROMISES ALIVE IN THE HEART

"To understand the immeasurable, the mind must be extraordinarily quiet, still."

Jiddu Krishnamurti

One tool that God gave to aid us to change things around us is the tool of meditation. In other words, you can call that principle of success. Many people have come to know the power behind meditation. Even in the business world, they understand the power of meditation and everyone is turning into this key. Most of the religions today that function in the world, is working by this principle. They teach their people to engage this tool to access the invisible realms.

Psychologists use it now. So, we can see that this principle is not just something for us to underestimate or overlook. You see, all these people developed that principle from the Word of God. They took it from the Word of God. But the truth is, many believers are carrying their Bibles, but they never look to see these principles God outlined for us. God left those promises for us to use and engage for prosperity and success. We are going to be foolish to ignore them.

When Joshua took over the leadership responsibility from Moses after his death, we can see how God taught him to be successful. So, in our walk with the Lord, this is the same principle we have to learn to engage. As we engage it, then we can harness the inherent energy in the promises of God. Let's look at the words here:

"This book of the law shall not depart out of thy mouth; but thou shalt meditate therein day and night, that thou mayest observe to do according to all that is written therein: for then thou shalt make thy way prosperous, and then thou shalt have good success." — *(Joshua 1:8)*

This is the key here. God told him that the book of the Lord (His promises) shall not depart from his mouth and he should meditate therein day and night and then obey and he is going to become successful. Success is predicated on this very principle—*the principle of meditation.* Engage this principle in your walk with the Lord and you are going to be amazed and stunned how much success is going to come your way.

This promise that God gave, wasn't only to Joshua. It was to you as well. The promise involved you and me. We have to practice it and then we can be able to experience the glory of the promises of God. Meditating on all that the Lord has promised can become a life-changer. Trust me, I know what I am talking about here. I have seen and experienced life in a "small way." So, I need you to engage this principle effectively.

This principle is so important that when Paul wrote his letter to his son, Timothy, he encouraged him of the same principle as well. We are going to be walking in the wrong way if we don't follow the advice as well. Remember that Paul wasn't just an ordinary man. He was a man who experienced the glory of his sonship. So, it is not a novice speaking here. It is one who had walked with the Lord and experienced the glory of that relationship. So, learn from it. Let's look at what he told his son:

"Neglect not the gift that is in thee, which was given thee by prophecy, with the laying on of the hands of the presbytery. Meditate upon these things; give thyself wholly to them; that thy profiting may appear to all." —(1 Timothy 4:14—15)

Paul is such a great father. He is showing this young man (and to us as well) the way to excellence and increase. He told him that all the prophecies (the promises) that were given to him, he should meditate on them. Then he stretched by saying, he should give himself wholly to them so that his profiting can appear. That means that the way to profit from the very things that concern the kingdom and its purposes is through meditation. Do you see the key now?

Meditation is the way to unlocking our profits. If we want to become effective and efficient in life, then we have to learn this very key.

Even as we conclude this book, I want you to know that you have to keep the promises of God alive in your heart. Whatever the Lord told you that you are going to become, you have to keep meditating on them. All that God promised you, keep pondering on them. As you are doing that, you are preparing yourself for your profiting. Our profiting from the very things God told us is in this very key— *meditation.*

Learn therefore to engage this very principle in your walk with the Lord. Meditation is one of the ways in which our faith comes alive. The more we spend time thinking and ruminating about something, it becomes part of us. Our realities become what we spend time thinking about. This is the asserting Solomon gave. He said that as a man thinks in his heart, so is he. That means, what you are pondering on, is what you become. If you spend time pondering on the promises of God, you become that which is promised.

If the Lord promised that you are going to become rich and you spend time meditating and taking action, you are going to become that. If the Lord told you that you are going to pastor a large ministry and you spend time meditating on it, and also acting out, then you are going to become that. If the Lord promised that you are going to have a glorious marriage and you spend time meditating on it, you are going to become that. If the Lord promised that you are going to become blessed in business and you spend time meditating on it and doing what is right, you become that.

What you mostly think about is what you are going to see. It is in this light I want to encourage you to spend time pondering on everything that the Lord told you. All that God has said to you; I want to encourage you to keep those promises alive in your heart. As you are thinking about them, you are creating the realities of those promises. Hallelujah!

"Blessed [is] the man that walketh not in the counsel of the ungodly, nor standeth in the way of sinners, nor sitteth in the seat of the scornful. But his delight [is] in the law of the Lord; and in his law doth he meditate day and night. And he shall be like a tree planted by the rivers of water, that bringeth forth his fruit in his season; his leaf also shall not wither; and whatsoever he doeth shall prosper." — (Psalms 1:1—3)

This is another text that unravels the power of meditation. God used metaphors here to describe the man who understands the way of meditation. He said he shall be like a tree that is planted by the rivers of water. Whew! This is just amazing. Just look at the choice of words. When one meditates on the law of God (God's promises) he is going to be ever productive and fruitful. No power of hell can undo this. It is what God has said.

Friend, as you walk with the Lord, whatever He has promised you, you have to learn to meditate. Keep all His promises alive in your heart. This is how things can increase your value and also success. Success gravitates towards this atmosphere. God Himself understands this very principle. He would not recommend this very principle if it never had the power to produce results. His words to Joshua confirm that assertion. He said that if he wanted to have good success, then he needed this principle of meditation. So, wisdom demands that you and I key into this counsel and then we can be able to maximize what God has promised us.

I want to encounter you next year by this time and you have become so great and bigger. How? That is, by you engaging this principle to the fullest. Make out some time and begin to engage this principle of mediating—especially, concerning the things God told you. This will invite the realm of increase and success to your side. Hallelujah!

Don't give up on the way even if it becomes tough. Keep the journey going. Keep meditating on the promises. Keep your mind focused on Him. Keep pondering on what He told you. Keep your faith alive in the promises of God. Everything He has said is going to come to pass without faith. There might be a delay, but it doesn't mean that He is not going to perform. He will and must deliver. Keep going. Keep believing. Keep focused and keep matching!

MY PRAYER FOR YOU!

My prayer for you is that you will not faint in the midst of the delay and lack. I pray that the Lord will grant you courage and the tenancy to keep moving towards the promises. It is my prayer no matter the circumstances that come your way, you will survive and will remain strong in the name of Jesus. As your days, so shall your strength be. No circumstances can overtake you. You will prosper in all that you do in the name of Jesus. The Lord shall be an everlasting light to guide your path in Jesus' name. Remain strong and prosper in all you do. Hallelujah!

SALVATION PRAYER:

If by the virtue of reading through this book you want to come to accept Jesus as your Lord and Savior or you want to rededicate your life again, I want you to pray with me and the Lord is going to restore you in every way.

"Dear Father, I acknowledge that I have sinned against You and I need your forgiveness. I ask that You forgive me and restore the glory of sonship over my life. Thank You that You sent Jesus to die for me. I declare that I am now a child of God and I have become a partaker of Your divine nature. Precious Holy Spirit, quicken me up to live for God in all holiness and truth. All the promises of God over the saints, I experience them forthwith in the name of Jesus. I declare I am the Lord's now and I have access to His presence and glory. Hallelujah!

Congratulations. If you have said this prayer, you are now born again and you are a child of God. What is needed is that you must grow in grace and the knowledge of Him. For this to happen, you need a local church where you can be taught the Word of God. We are going to be glad to have you part of our church family. Get in touch today. Or you find a Bible-believing church near you to fellowship with them. God bless you as you do. We will be glad to hear from you. contact us on the following:

+44 (0) 208 357 9801

+44 (0) 793 921 3236

+44 (0) 795 855 7905

Info@newgloryinternational.com

lolaosikoya@hotmail.co.uk

ABOUT THE BOOK:

Life brings us diverse challenges each day. The problem is that when many people face this, they begin to lose faith and confidence in God. We are in a time where the world is going through crises and diverse challenges. There are economic, social, Spiritual, financial, marriage, and even business crises all over the world now. In the midst of these crises, many people turn to lose their faith in God. Instead of believing, many focus on the challenges—(From introduction)

In this Masterpeice, Senior Pastor Lola Osikoya challenges your mind to trust in God regardless of what you are going through life. She brings you to understand:

- *God rewards faith*
- *How you can learn the concept of faith*
- *That circumstances cannot dethrone God*
- *How to keep focused on God instead*
- *You are heavenly aided— and there is no need to fret*
- *The assured promises*
- *How to keep the promises alive in the heart*

Filled with inspired throughts and experiential realities, she aims to strengthen your faith so that you can attain the reward of your faith. Faith has rewards. Hence, we must learn to see beyond our cirucumstances so we can experience those rewards inherent in faith.

ABOUT THE AUTHOR

Senior Pastor Lola Osikoya is the lead Minister of the New Glory International Ministries based in the United Kingdom. She has served the Lord from her childhood and God has gloriously used her tremendously to challenge lives and redirect the destinies of men alike into their purpose in Christ.

She is a grandmother and an anointed minister of the Gospel whose ministry has challenged many to purpose. She is a conference speaker, revivalist and also a teacher of the Word of God. Through her conferences and telecast programs, many lives have been changed and challenged to purpose.

Printed in Great Britain
by Amazon

71178585R00059